The Enchanted Cat
2007 COVR AWARD WINNER in the
Best Book Magick/Shamanism Category

Cottage Witchery
"This is the perfect book to have around if you want to
make every area of your home magical."
—*NewWitch* (4 broomsticks)

Natural Witchery
2008 COVR AWARD WINNER in the
Best Book Wicca/Paganism Category

"Interspersed throughout the text are lively anecdotes from
Dugan's own Samantha Stephens-esque household. The
value of this book lies in the warm, personal touch Dugan
uses both in her writing and in her craft."
—*Publishers Weekly*

"Her primer for 'green' witchcraft—i.e., witchcraft in tune
with seasonal elements—is a gold mine of concepts and resources for the novice to intermediate practitioner. Chock-
full of relevant wisdom and lively humor, this is a valuable
addition to any avid pagan's personal reference library."
—*Library Journal*

Ellen Dugan, also known as the Garden Witch, is a psychic-clairvoyant who lives in Missouri with her husband and three children. A practicing Witch for over twenty years, Ellen also has many years of nursery and garden center experience, including landscape and garden design. She received her Master Gardener status through the University of Missouri and her local county extension office. Look for other articles by Ellen in Llewellyn's annual *Magical Almanac*, *Witches' Calendar*, *Witches' Datebook*, and *Witches' Spell-A-Day Almanac*. Visit her website at:

www.ellendugan.com

HERB MAGIC
for Beginners

Down-to-Earth Enchantments

Ellen Dugan

Llewellyn Publications
Woodbury, Minnesota

First Edition
Fourth Printing, 2009

Cover images by Elizabeth Dowle © Quarto, Inc.
Cover design by Adrienne W. Zimiga
Edited by Andrea Neff
Llewellyn is a registered trademark of Llewellyn Worldwide, Ltd.

Cataloging-in-Publication Data is on file with the Library of Congress.
ISBN 13: 978-0-7387-0837-9
ISBN 10: 0-7387-0837-2

Llewellyn Publications
A Division of Llewellyn Worldwide, Ltd.
2143 Wooddale Drive, Dept. 978-0-7387-0837-9
Woodbury, Minnesota 55125-2989, U.S.A.
www.llewellyn.com

Printed in the United States of America

Other Books by Ellen Dugan

Garden Witchery: Magick from the Ground Up
(Llewellyn Publications, 2003)

Elements of Witchcraft: Natural Magick for Teens
(Llewellyn Publications, 2003)

*7 Days of Magic: Spells, Charms & Correspondences for the
Bewitching Week*
(Llewellyn Publications, 2004)

Cottage Witchery: Natural Magick for Hearth and Home
(Llewellyn Publications, 2005)

Autumn Equinox: The Enchantment of Mabon
(Llewellyn Publications, 2005)

The Enchanted Cat: Feline Fascinations, Spells & Magick
(Llewellyn Publications, 2006)

Natural Witchery: Intuitive, Personal & Practical Magick
(Llewellyn Publications, 2007)

How to Enchant a Man: Spells to Bewitch, Bedazzle & Beguile
(Llewellyn Publications, 2008)

*Book of Witchery: Spells, Charms & Correspondences
for Every Day of the Week*
(Llewellyn Publications, 2009)

Garden Witch's Herbal: Green Magick, Herbalism & Spirituality
(Llewellyn Publications, 2009)

Note about Herbs

The herbs listed in this book are to be used in charms and spells. They are not intended to treat medical problems. Also, if you have sensitive skin, wear gardening gloves while gathering the plants. Some lovely garden herbs, like heliotrope, can cause skin irritation. Keep poison-control information in a handy spot, just in case. The National Poison Control hotline number (for adults and children) is 1-800-222-1222. Bottom line: use common sense. Be aware that anything can cause an allergic reaction. If you are not sure what the herb is, leave it alone, and for Goddess' sake, don't eat it!

In no way is this material a substitute for trained medical or psychological care. This book is intended to be used by stable, mature adults seeking personal awareness and transformation. All herbal formulas are given for historic understanding and reference. No herbal formula should be consumed unless specifically stated. Herbs and herbal formulas that are potentially toxic are stated, and the author and publisher assume no responsibility for those who consume such preparations in any dose. People with allergies or sensitive skin should take caution when using herbal remedies. Do not take any herb or herbal preparation without direct consultation from a qualified health care provider.

Contents

Contents

Contents

Spells

Spells

Acknowledgments

Thanks to all of the friends and relatives, too numerous to mention, who bring me old gardening and antique herb books because they figured I could use them eventually—and I usually do. To Paula, Gwen, Heather, Nicole, and Colleen, who put up with me when I need to bounce ideas off of them.

A very special thank you to Sandy, who unselfishly turned me loose in her library and allowed me to borrow her herb books. To Christopher, for the good advice and great tips for reference materials, and most importantly for reminding me to write about "what I teach and what I love."

Thanks to Natalie Harter and Nancy Mostad, in Llewellyn's acquisitions department, for asking if I would be interested in this project to begin with.

Also, a long overdue thanks goes to Scott Killpack, the head cheese of the local University Outreach and Extension Center and of my Master Gardeners. Thanks, Scott, for the cheerful and on-the-spot responses to any plant question I couldn't find the answer to.

Lastly, thanks to my husband, Ken, and our three children, Kraig, Kyle, and Erin. I love you guys!

He who knows what sweets and virtues are in the ground,
the waters, the plants, the heavens, and how to come at these
enchantments, is the rich and royal man.

—RALPH WALDO EMERSON

Though leaves are many, the root is one . . .
—WILLIAM BUTLER YEATS

INTRODUCTION

GOING BACK TO MY MAGICAL ROOTS

When I first decided to write a book on the topic of herb magic for beginners, I wasn't really sure where to begin. I stalled and procrastinated for a time, and then made up my mind to take a look back at my own beginnings, hoping for a little inspiration. Perhaps if I took a trip to my past and went back to my Witchy roots, I would find the motivation

I needed. So, I pulled out my oldest books and notes and had a wonderful time sentimentally leafing through my first magical journal, or Book of Shadows. There, in a three-ring binder on loose-leaf notebook paper, was the record of my first herbal research, and magical experiences.

As I flipped through my journal and through the battered pages of my earliest books, I felt a quiet glow of contentment inside of me. Some of my first magical books (which were all, oddly enough, on herb magic) continue to be my favorites today, even though these paperback reference materials are showing the signs of being well used for almost twenty years. A few of my books are so well loved that the pages fall out if you open them too wide, and the edges of the covers are dog-eared and worn from countless openings and closings. While newer editions with snazzier covers are available, I would never consider trading mine in. For there are memories here . . . magical ones.

This trip down memory lane helped me recall that first rush of wonder and enthusiasm I felt for the topic of magical herbs and plants. It also offered me a little insight into myself and how I have evolved as both a Witch and a woman. On one rainy October afternoon, I rediscovered how truly exciting and awesome it is to learn about a magical topic for the first time. I felt that little spark that writers feel when they suddenly know how to turn an idea into a book. My inspiration came from my old journals, where I found aged, pressed leaves of various herbs tucked in the handwritten pages, and my children's sweet, crayon-colored drawings from when they were small. I sat and chuckled at my earliest attempts at composing my own herbal spells, and at how truly horrific and melodramatic some of the rhymes and charms were. But, being a Virgo, I had kept track of all the results, and bad prose or not, my herbal spells had garnered results, every time.

As I went to put the journal away, a pressed leaf fluttered to the floor. I scooped it up and found that it was a preserved sage leaf. The aroma was faint, but it made me chuckle at the very appropriate symbolism. For this is the herb used to promote wisdom, and I knew absolutely that it was time for me to reawaken my herbal knowledge—to breathe some new life into herb folklore and plant wisdom, and to share it with others.

I admit that I have a passion for the natural world and a love affair with green, growing things. The very word *herb* has always seemed to me to be a fascinating one. After all, there is something mysterious about herbs, and their uses, aromas, tastes, and textures. Their histories and folklores are captivating, and for many Witches the topic of magical herbalism is an irresistible one. The late author Scott Cunningham called magical herbalism "the secret craft of the wise." While I don't really think it's so much a *secret* these days, it is an important part of our magical heritage. Let's get back to our roots and study this topic from a fresh perspective.

It is my hope that this book for beginners will inspire other magic users with the same rush of wonder, mystery, and enchantment that herbs have always invoked in me.

Open your heart and connect to the earth. Respect the power and energies of the many bewitching herbal plants and trees. Magic is in everything, all around you. It takes only an open mind and an accepting heart to discover it.

Man did not weave the web of life: he is merely a strand in it.
Whatever he does to the web, he does to himself.

—CHIEF SEATTLE

CHAPTER ONE

WHAT IS HERB MAGIC?

Magic is the art of effecting positive change in your life. Magic is also a force of nature that is, as yet, unexplained by science. In truth, all of nature is interconnected, like the shimmering strands of a spider's web. If you touch one part of the web, the entire thing will vibrate. Each and every one of the world's religions were woven on this spiritual web, and all of creation and nature are interconnected. One way of connecting to this web of life is through the practice of magic. For as we perform magic and cast our spells to bring about positive change, we are gently weaving new patterns into the spiritual web.

Magic is a sympathetic process. It works on the basis of your own personal power and a connection, vibration, or *harmony* between things. Magic revolves around the essence of life, the power of the four natural elements of earth, air, fire, and water, and a reverence for the natural world. This respect for the life force and empathy with green, growing things are at the very heart of all magical practice.

Herb magic is a natural way to experience this mystery. To work herb magic, you must first understand the elemental powers in plant life and get to know the bewitching abilities of these aromatic plants. The powers that live in an herb are determined by the plant's growing habits, and its scent, color, texture, and shape. Take a good look at the plants growing in your garden. What can you learn about them through your sense of touch? For example, what do the prickly leaves of the thistle tell you? What does the shape of the holly leaf remind you of? The answers to these magical questions are both simple and profound.

According to herbal tradition, both thistle and holly leaf are protective plants. Because they are associated with the element of fire and the planet Mars, they carry strong, forceful qualities, a type of warrior energy, just as the Roman god Mars did. Plants that have a planetary correspondence to

Mars tend to be used for protective purposes. The thistle is a classic protective, Witch's garden plant. Its spiny stems and leaves ward away intruders and protect the bearer from melancholy.

Holly leaves have the charming folk name of "bat wings," and if you take a good look at the spiny leaves, you can see how the leaves have a bat-wing look. The holly shrub (yes, it is also an herb) protects the home from lightning and is often incorporated into midwinter festivities, as it is an evergreen plant and symbolizes life, good luck, and renewal. These are just a few examples of the magic and folklore of herbal plants. The truth is that there is much more to herbs than you might imagine.

By studying the path of the magical herbalist, you will be uncovering older plant folklore and knowledge. This herb-garden path is in fact a well-worn road, made smooth and peaceful by the wisdom and healing traditions of the many women and men who blazed the trail for us so long ago. Herb magic gives us the opportunity to work hand in hand with nature. Here, as we grow our herbs in pots and containers, or tend to them in our backyard gardens, we are joined by the spirits of the Wise Ones throughout time.

So, consider this your chance to acquaint yourself with one of the oldest forms of folk wisdom and magic. Plan on spending some time outdoors, reconnecting to nature. Take a good look around and discover all of the magic and mystery that the natural world and plant kingdom have to offer you. There was a time when all plant life was considered sacred, magical, and important to humans. Today, herbs present us with a rewarding combination of beauty, enchantment, and usefulness.

What Is an Herb?

The definition of an herb has changed over the centuries. Once upon a time, it meant "grass, green crops, and leafy plants." Today, an herb is understood to be a plant that is used for medicine, food, flavoring, or scent. Any part of the plant—the roots, stem, bark, leaves, fruits, seeds, or flowers—may be used for such purposes. An herb may be a tree, shrub, woody perennial, flower, annual, or fern.

Herbs are a varied and multipurpose group of plants that have been valued throughout time for their many culinary, healing, and magical uses. In days past, they were the main source for medicines, dietary supplements, and, of course, culinary seasonings. Herbs also fulfilled a wide variety of household needs. They provided fragrance in the home, were mixed into beauty and bath preparations, were used as cleaning agents, and were used to dye cloth and to repel insects.

Today, herbs are cultivated as culinary herbs, to flavor dishes and meals. They are grown for their beauty, form, and history. They can also be grown ornamentally to create a type of magical garden. In these magical places, herbal flowers, plants, trees, and shrubs are grown together to encourage an atmosphere of enchantment. They are grown and tended to provide supplies for spellcasting, and to help create a serene and sacred outdoor space.

Where to Find Your Herbal Materials

To begin, you can try growing your own herbs. Magic works in harmony with nature. See what you can learn by tending plants and following the natural cycles of the growing season. You can consider incorporating into your spells and charms many varieties of blooming plants that are also classified as herbs. A few examples include the pansy, peony, and rose, but there are dozens of others of which you may be unaware (although I'm aiming to fix that for you in very short order). Also, we'll take a look here at a few types of trees that are commonly available, such as the sugar maple, silver birch, willow, and oak. Surprise! These are all classified as herbal trees.

Pick up some starter herb packs at the nursery or garden center this year, and pot them in pretty containers. Place these on a sunny windowsill or porch, and see how they do for you. Or you could really live on the edge and plant them outside in the garden. Check out the little tags that come with your garden plants and herbs for instructions on how to plant and care for them. However, there are some good gardening practices every magical herbalist should follow, and it certainly would benefit you to add the following practical information to your repertoire.

Gardening Tips:
The Three S's—Site, Soil, and Sun

The love of gardening is a seed that once sown never dies.

—GERTRUDE JEKYLL

Site

Do your homework and know your area. What cold hardiness zone do you live in? What is your lowest average temperature in the winter? Will the plants you are considering survive your winter lows or your summer highs? Is your garden easy to get to? Can you climb around the garden, or will it be difficult to maintain? Can you water it easily, or will you have to drag out a garden hose?

Soil

What is your soil like? Is it clay or loam? Rocky or sandy? Contact your local university extension office and the local chapter of Master Gardener volunteers and get some practical gardening information and soil tips for your area. Always add some organic material, such as compost, to your garden, and work it in. This will bump up the nutrient level of your soil, and your plants will thank you.

Sun

Know your garden and the sun and shade patterns. Every yard will be unique. Make a map of your sun and shade patterns and then add your plants accordingly ("the right plant in the right place"). Sun-loving plants will sulk in too much shade. Likewise, shade-loving plants will fry in too much sun. Read the plant tags and follow the recommended sun requirements. If the sun tolerance doesn't work out, move the plant to a better location.

Gathering Live Herbs for Magical Use: Do's and Don'ts

Now that I've piqued your curiosity, let's discuss how to gather your herb materials from the garden. Just as with any other type of enchantment, there are some friendly and earth-conscious rules and guidelines to consider while gathering live herbs for magic.

Gathering Do's

- Harm none.
- Do use a sharp knife or pair of garden scissors.
- Do cut the leaves or stems cleanly.
- Do pay back the plant with fertilizer and care.
- Do know how to identify poison ivy, oak, and sumac.
- Do take a tree-identification guidebook along if you are looking for leaves.
- Do leave the area looking better than you found it.
- Do take the smallest amount of plant material possible, no more than an eighth of the plant. It's not the quantity that counts in magic—it's the *quality.*
- Do say a charm over the plant while you gather the herb (see the following).

A Gathering Charm

Whenever you go to gather your live plant material, be it blossom, leaf, or bud, enchant or bless the herb by saying a charm over it. This is a traditional part of gathering plant material for spellwork. All of nature is sacred, and a plant's life force should be respected. The following verse is a quick and easy charm to memorize, and better yet, it's an all-purpose one. Try it out.

I gather this herb for a magic spell, bringing harm to none.
May it turn out well.

Gathering Don'ts

- Don't snitch flowers and herbs from someone else's private garden, or from a public garden.

- Don't take wildflowers or gather plant material from a park. Some species are protected, so you could be fined. You should leave the plants undisturbed for everyone to enjoy.

- Don't skulk around in the dark; this will not add to the mystique. Because you can't see what you're doing, you could gather the wrong plant or nip a finger.

- Don't break or twist off stems or twigs from plants and trees. Follow some basic pruning rules and cut them away cleanly.

- Don't medicate yourself or your children with herbs. Always consult a qualified, licensed herbalist or physician concerning health issues.

- Don't be foolish. The herbs listed in this book are to be used in charms and spells. They are not intended to treat medical problems. Also, if you have sensitive skin, wear gardening gloves while gathering the plants. Some lovely garden herbs, like heliotrope, can cause skin irritation. Keep poison-control information in a handy spot, just in case. The National Poison Control hotline number (for adults and children) is 1-800-222-1222. Bottom line: use common sense. Be aware that *anything* can cause an allergic reaction. If you are not sure what the herb is, leave it alone, and for Goddess' sake, don't eat it!

More Options for "Gathering" Herbs: Hit the Stores or Dig in Your Spice Rack

If you do not have the space to grow your own herbal materials, there are other options available to you. Check out the produce section of the grocery store or a specialty cooking store. Many produce sections have a selection of fresh culinary herbs, such as parsley, mint, sage, thyme, basil, and rosemary. All of these herbs are indeed magical plants.

Or, dare to dig around in your spice rack in the kitchen, and try working with dried culinary herbs and spices. Add a pinch of cinnamon to a spell to increase prosperity, a bit of garlic to repel negativity, sage for wisdom, cloves for protection, and so on. There are dozens of cooking spices that are also magical herbs. And yes, we'll get into those in the later theme chapters—I won't leave you hanging. By the time you are finished with this book, you'll never look at plants, herbs, or spices the same way again.

Also, many metaphysical shops carry a selection of dried herbs. Make sure you label them, note any toxic information, and date what you buy. Store these dried herbs in airtight, nonporous glass jars (old sterilized canning jars are ideal for this). Keep the jars out of direct sunlight, and don't keep dried magical herbs for more than a year. If you end up storing your magical herbs in the kitchen, make sure you keep them well away from your cooking and seasoning spices, so there are no mix-ups. Better safe than sorry.

How Herb Magic Works

The universe is full of magical things
patiently waiting for our wits to grow sharper.
—EDEN PHILLPOTTS

So, how does this stuff all work, anyway? Well, herb magic works according to several magical principles. It works because the Witch or magic user taps into and directs the energy and power naturally inherent within the plants while also tapping into and directing his or her own personal power. All living things have an essence, a life force, or an *energy*, if you will. This force has a specific vibration or power. Each of these herbal energies is subtly different from another. Some herbs promote love, others encourage protection, and so on. Now, when the magician draws upon her own personal power, focuses her intention on a positive goal, and combines her knowledge of the herbal energies, this creates herb magic. Essentially, you know what change or goal you want, you do the work, and then you allow yourself to reap the benefits.

You will find that all of the herbal spells and charms in this book are positive ones. There are chapters that focus specifically on the topics of herb magic for love and happiness, health, prosperity, and protection. But before you begin to cast your first herbal spells, you need to ask yourself a few important questions. This is a way of checking to make sure that the changes that you are considering will respect others and cause no harm. Taking the time to reflect on your planned herb magic separates the dabbler from the serious practitioner.

Magic is a divine act in which we seek to create loving change, not to stir up chaos and trouble. Remember that spiritual web we discussed earlier? It is important to reflect on and be considerate of the entire cosmic web, and not just the tiny part you are in. That way, you can be sure your magic will be a positive, life-affirming, and effective use of your personal power. With that in mind, study the following rules of magic.

The Basic Rules of Magic

Intention

Here is where we separate the dabbler from the magician. What is your intention? Is it a positive one that harms none and takes into consideration the free will of others? If you are trying to whip up an herbal spell to make that guy or girl of your dreams fall hopelessly in love with you, you are definitely looking for trouble. Try working to make yourself more attractive instead. If you are looking for a raise or promotion at your job, work hard and then perform magic on yourself to catch the attention of your boss in a positive way. Cast your herbal spell for good luck and career advancement and to make yourself seem savvier and more promotion-worthy, but don't go and hex your co-workers who are also trying for the promotion. Talk about your bad mojo. You can climb the corporate ladder without stepping on others. Be creative, and most of all, be conscientious. Targeting a specific individual, whether in a love spell or to win out over that person, is manipulation. So be honest with yourself and carefully consider your goals. Now, take a few moments to ground and center and to put aside all negative emotions.

Grounding and Centering

Take a deep breath and ground yourself. Visualize all the stress and negative emotions you carry draining away harmlessly into the earth. Now take a deep breath, and slowly blow it out. Then reach down and put your hands on the ground. Imagine that tree roots are growing from the soles of your bare feet and down into the rich soil. Stay there for a moment and then draw up some positive earth energy. Keep up those nice, slow, deep breaths. Picture yourself as a plant that draws sustenance and strength from the earth. Stand up and reach your fingers up to the sky. Gently stretch yourself out and up, and wiggle your fingers. (I like to imagine that my fingers are like the leaves on a tree. Try it for yourself—it always makes me smile.) Just enjoy the feeling of being connected to the earth, while all that steady, nurturing energy streams through you. Lower your arms, and take in a deep breath. Hold it for a count of four, then slowly release it by blowing gently out through your mouth. Now that you feel refreshed and energized by the stabilizing powers of the earth, you are good to go.

The Law of Three

You should be aware of the magical Law of Three, which says that whatever energies you send out will be returned to you in kind—times three. This is a metaphysical way of saying, "What goes around, comes around." Therefore, it makes absolutely no sense to perform negative spells, as the magic is just going to circle around back to you, with a vengeance. So, as conscientious magic users, our intentions must be positive and our magic must be worked in the best way possible for all those involved.

Respect Yourself and Others

The basic law of Wicca and affirmative magic is "Harm none." This is a fundamental rule that is not open to interpretation or change. Another important aspect of magic is keeping your magic free of manipulation. Taking away another's free will definitely causes harm, so consider your options carefully before you cast a spell. You can also hedge your bets, so to speak, by including a closing line to your herbal spells. This tag line reinforces your magic and ensures that the best possible outcome will occur.

A Closing Line for Your Herbal Spells

Here is a good all-purpose closing line, sometimes referred to as a tag line (because you "tag" it on at the end). You can add this to all your herbal spells and charms.

For the good of all, with harm to none.
By herb magic this spell is done.

Here's Something Else to Consider: Herb Magic Is a Major Magic

A "major magic" is defined as one that requires a higher level of expertise and knowledge. Herb magics fall in this category. So, while this is a book designed for learning the basics of herb magic, you should know that you will be combining many different aspects of traditional magic into the study of magical herbalism. Pretty cool, huh?

The complexity of the subject matter held me up on the writing of this book for a while. How was I to teach magical herbalism to a beginner, when it isn't necessarily a beginner's topic? I absolutely refused to dummy it down, so that left me with the option of telling it like it is and going from there. While you perform your herbal spells and charms, you will be utilizing other types of magics, such as color magic, planetary symbols, candle magic, and astrological timing. All of these different techniques are often incorporated into herb magic.

The bottom line is that there is much more to the topic of herb magic than meets the eye. You have to study and practice this variety of magic in order to become proficient at it, but it is really enjoyable to experiment with and perform herbal spells. It's a sensory experience—there is nothing like getting your hands into something and discovering the scents, textures, and energies of the various herbs for yourself. I do recommend that you keep detailed notes of your herbal charms and spells. (We'll talk more about this in the last chapter.) This will help you as you learn and grow in the traditional art of magical herbalism.

The next section covers the basic elements of spellcasting This is a fundamental outline for working magic, and it is included here for you to study and then apply to your own personalized brand of enchantment.

The Elements of Spellwork

The majority of Witches, magical herbalists, and other magic users will agree that there are several elements to the successful performance of a ritual or spell. While people's opinions on how to cast a spell may vary, the essentials remain the same. Inspect the following list, and you'll get the idea.

Purpose

Take a moment to center your focus and calm your mind. Now ask yourself the following questions: What do I *really* need from this herbal spell? What is the goal of the spell or charm? How can I best work my herb magic for a positive outcome that will harm none? Mull this over for a bit, and write down your magical goals if necessary. Take your time, and mentally prepare yourself to work the spell.

Sequence

Every spell, charm, ritual, or act of magic has a clear beginning and end. Write up a quick outline to help you sort things out. You may find it helpful to refer to the "Herbal Spell Worksheet" on pages 164–165. Set things up, and get ready to cast your spell.

Sacred Space

Establishing sacred space when you work your magic is an excellent idea. Choose a clean, happy, and pleasant environment in which to cast your spells. Call on the God and Goddess to assist you. This is a simple step, and one that is often overlooked. Just ask them in your own words to bless your work area and to help you create a sacred space. No muss, no fuss. By the way, your working area doesn't have to be fancy or elaborate. Try keeping things natural and simple. You could toss a scarf over a table, sit on the floor, or work your magic at a special spot like your household shrine or altar. Or maybe you'd prefer to cast your herb magic while sitting under a tree in your backyard. Wherever you choose to work, invite the God and Goddess to assist you, and take the time and effort to create a special and sacred space.

Supplies

All spellcraft and magic employ supplies of some sort. In this book, we will, of course, be focusing on herbs. However, as mentioned earlier, colored candles, swatches of fabric, colored ribbons, and other props are often incorporated into herb magic. You will want to select materials that will work well together, and toward the goal you have in mind. These complementary items will enhance and personalize your herb magic. We will discuss these tools in more detail in chapter 2.

Timing

Astrological timing plays a huge role in magic of any form. One of the simplest methods is following the magical correspondences that are assigned to each day of the week. Every day of the week, Sunday through Saturday, has its own special magical energy that can be incorporated into your herbal spells. There are also a few other options available to you when it comes to magical timing. One is to consider the various seasons of the year. Use the spring season for growth, energy, and new beginnings, and the summer months for passion, fertility, and power. Consider the fall months for prosperity, abundance, harvest, and balance, and the winter for protection, rest, study, and meditation. Another timing option is to consider the phases of the moon. Work in the waxing moon to pull things toward you, in the full moon for extra power, and in the waning moon to push things away. In the next chapter, we will discuss the days of the week and the moon and her magics in much more detail.

Creativity and Imagination

This last element of spellcasting is, of course, the most important one. You should feel free to take the information from this book and others, and apply it in new and original ways to your herb magic. Refer to the correspondence charts in the appendix of this book, and learn the basics. Then, use your imagination to conjure up your own unique herbal spells and charms. I've said it before, but it bears repeating: magic is where you find it, and creativity is the key.

Nature, the Ultimate Teacher

Go forth, under the open sky, and list to Nature's teachings.

—WILLIAM CULLEN BRYANT

Let's dig into some more practical herb magic tips. In our next chapter, there are secrets and symbols, plus some terminology you'll need to know, and the tools of the herbalist's trade. Are you ready to begin? I bet you are planning and plotting out all sorts of wonderful charms and spells to try.

The study of herbalism is the perfect excuse to get back into the natural world, where you belong. (Yes, it's my goal in life to get Witches and magic users off the couch or away from their computers for a while.) It's a magical thing to feel the earth beneath your bare feet, to feel an affinity with nature and all the green, growing plants. Nature is the ultimate teacher. If you show her some respect and listen closely, you'll be amazed at what you will discover and what magical things you will learn.

*The whole secret of the study of nature
lies in learning how to use one's eyes.*

—GEORGE SAND

CHAPTER TWO

HERB MAGIC SECRETS:
TIMING, TERMS, AND TOOLS
OF THE TRADE

Now that we've gone over the basics of herb magic and spellwork, let's get into the secrets and insider tricks that will help you combine all of this information and get your herb magic up and rolling. We mentioned astrological and lunar timing briefly before, but the subject does deserve a better explanation. Each day of the week is aligned with a specific planet, a color or colors, a magical specialty, and a magical energy. Getting to know the basic correspondences and magical themes for each day of the week—and their accompanying herbs—is a nifty little technique to add to your magical repertoire. This is a traditional form of magic, as herbs and astrology have been combined successfully for centuries.

The astrological information presented here is based only on the planetary influences of the days of the week. Otherwise it gets a little too confusing, even for me. Hey, I'm not afraid to admit that complicated astrological jargon is way over my head. So no worries—this is basic information. The following section breaks down the data for you in an easy-to-read daily format.

The planetary influence for the day of the week is given first, followed by a list of enchantments that correspond with that particular day. Next, the colors that correspond to that specific day of the week are given. Use this color information to coordinate candles, or to choose fabric to make herbal charm bags. Finally, a few of the common herbs that align with the daily planetary energy are listed.

Basically, this is a handy-dandy correspondence chart and a daily reference guide for your herb magic. You will find it much easier to create your own herbal spells and charms, as you'll know immediately what things complement each other, and which accessories work well together.

Days of the Week and Their
Herb Magic Correspondences

Sunday

Planetary influence—The Sun

Symbol— ☉

Cast for—Success, realizing your goals, building confidence, wealth, fame

Candle/charm bag colors—Yellow and gold

Common herbs associated with the Sun—Ash tree, bay, cinnamon, heliotrope, juniper, orange peel, St. John's wort, witch hazel

Monday

Planetary influence—The Moon

Symbol— ☽

Cast for—Goddess magic, women's mysteries, emotions, instincts, intuition

Candle/charm bag colors—White and silver

Common herbs associated with the Moon—Aloe, eucalyptus, lemon rind, mallow, myrrh, sandalwood, wintergreen

Tuesday

Planetary influence—Mars

Symbol— ♂

Cast for—Problem solving, courage, passion, vitality

Candle/charm bag colors—Red and black

Common herbs associated with Mars—Allspice, chili pepper, coriander, dragon's blood, garlic, holly, nettle, pepper, thistle

Wednesday

Planetary influence—Mercury

Symbol— ☿

Cast for—Communication matters, cleverness, creativity, to improve your luck

Candle/charm bag colors—Orange or purple

Common herbs associated with Mercury—Almond, celery seed, dill, fennel, lavender, parsley

Thursday

Planetary influence—Jupiter

Symbol— ♃

Cast for—Prosperity, expansion, moving up in the world, healing and health

Candle/charm bag colors—Green, purple, and royal blue

Common herbs associated with Jupiter—Anise, borage, clove, hyssop, maple, nutmeg, oak, sage

Friday

Planetary influence—Venus

Symbol— ♀

Cast for—Love, luxury, pleasure, entertainment

Candle/charm bag colors—Pink and aqua green

Common herbs associated with Venus—Catnip, elder, feverfew, foxglove, iris, orris root, periwinkle, tansy, thyme, valerian, vervain, violet

Saturday

Planetary influence—Saturn

Symbol— ♄

Cast for—Protection, banishing, bindings

Candle/charm bag colors—Black or deep purple

Common herbs associated with Saturn—Comfrey, elm, ivy, mimosa, morning glory, mullein, pansy, patchouli, poplar, quince, yew

Lunar Timing and Herb Magic

Observe due measure, for right timing is in all things the most important factor.

—HESIOD

You are probably wondering why I'm focusing so much on timing when it comes to herb magic. Well, the truth is that timing plays an essential role in all of magic. We began this chapter by taking a look at the days of the week, but we should also consider the moon and her bewitching phases. The moon holds more power over our magic than any other object in the sky. One of the simplest ways to add a little oomph to your herb magic is to work in harmony with the lunar cycles. Working in accord with the lunar phases ensures that your charms and spells turn out the way you want them to.

Over the years, I have found that I divide the lunar phases into five categories: new, waxing, full, waning, and the dark of the moon. There are specific magical applications for each of these phases, and once you have the essentials down, you can use these lunar associations alone or in combination with the daily correspondences for an unbeatable combination.

New Moon

The new moon is the beginning of the lunar cycle. This phase begins on the last day of the "dark of the moon" phase. The following evening, if you are observant, you will probably see that very thin crescent, low in the western sky. Cast your herbal spells during the new moon phase for new beginnings, birth, growth, and fresh starts.

Waxing Moon

The waxing moon is technically when the moon is in the first quarter and second quarter phases. Every evening, you'll notice that the moon is higher and higher in the western sky at sunset. As it rolls farther into the second quarter, it seems to begin to rise in the east an hour or so before sunset. Traditionally, you cast spells and create charms during the waxing moon for "increase" and to draw positive things and goals toward you. A few of these positive goals may include fertility, creativity, health and wellness, prosperity, happiness, and love.

Full Moon

The full moon rises in the east, just at sunset. The full moon phase is technically the day before the full moon, the day of the full moon, and the day after. This is an incredibly powerful time, so when you need to pull out all the stops, work your herb magic during the full moon. The full moon is an *all-purpose* lunar phase, as we'll discuss in the later theme chapters.

Waning Moon

The waning moon begins the day after the full moon, with the advent of the third quarter moon phase, and on into the fourth quarter. The moon rises a little later in the eastern sky each evening, and you will notice that it begins to look slightly lopsided. As each night progresses, the right side of the moon looks a bit more pared down. Work during this lunar phase to push away unwanted energies and to remove negative situations. Now is when you cast herbal spells for "decrease" and to banish. (As the moon shrinks, so does the problem.) Use this phase to drive out illness or fatigue or to banish dread or fear. This is also a great time to cleanse and to send negativity out of your life and your home.

Dark of the Moon

Technically, this phase occurs during the last two days of the fourth lunar phase and on the actual day of the new moon. These are the days when the moon is not visible in the night sky. I have read in various books over the years that this is supposedly a "dangerous" lunar phase and that you should not cast any spells or perform any magics during this time. I strongly disagree. Who started this nonsense anyway?

The moon is an enchanting symbol for the Goddess in all her aspects: the Maiden for the increasing crescent, the Mother for the full moon, and the Crone for the waning moon. Yes, it is true that working in the dark of the moon requires planning and wisdom on your part. But if you carefully plot out your magics and work with good judgment, you can achieve wondrous results. This phase is the best time to work to remove very negative situations. I have had phenomenal success working in the dark of the moon with protection magic. You can work at this time to keep prowlers away, to remove ghosts, to protect your property, and even to banish stalkers.

Moon Goddesses and Lunar Herbs

If you'd like to connect to the power of the moon goddesses while working your herb magic during the various moon phases, take a look at this classic trinity of Greco-Roman lunar goddesses and some of their associated plants.

Artemis

Artemis is a Maiden who is often referred to as a virgin; this term denotes that she belonged to herself. It was rumored that Artemis had lovers both male and female, but according to mythology, her lovers usually met with a sad end. Artemis and her Roman counterpart, Diana, are associated with the waxing crescent moon. This divine huntress is called on to assist in childbirth, to protect women from violence, for courage, and for daring to be yourself and walking your own path. She is associated with the following lunar herbs: daisy, date palm, myrtle, and mugwort. Mugwort's botanical name is *Artemisia*—isn't that interesting? Artemis is also associated with the herbal trees hazel, willow, and cypress.

Selene

Selene, also called Luna in the Roman pantheon, is the Mother aspect and goddess of the full moon. This divine enchantress is invoked for *any* type of affirmative magic, as she is extremely fond of magic users and Witches in general. Selene is known for her quick, subtle, and common-sense magical assistance. She is associated with these lunar herbs: a white fully open rose, bluebells, and honesty. The botanical name for honesty is *Lunaria*, another nifty name tie-in. Selene is also associated with the night-blooming jasmine vine and the moonflower vine. Please note that the moonflower vine, while a lovely night-blooming plant, is mildly toxic and should be kept out of reach of children.

Hecate

Hecate, the Crone, is a Greco-Roman goddess and a guardian and patron of Witches. She is wise and all-seeing. Hecate is a triple goddess, and has three faces. Just to keep things interesting, she may appear as a lovely young woman, an attractive matron, or a wise, silver-haired old Crone. Call on Hecate for wisdom, knowledge, and protection. Hecate is associated with these herbs: mint, cyclamen, dandelion, and garlic. She is also associated with the oak and willow trees, as well as many poisonous herbal plants, such as aconite (also known as wolfsbane), belladonna, hemlock, and mandrake.

These last four herbs are noted for interest only. All are very poisonous. Sometimes you will see poisonous herbs listed as being "baneful," an old term that means basically "herbs that will cause death." So think about it before you go and hunt down some of those old plants because you think it sounds cool to have them sitting around. They do not add to the atmosphere. You're not going to impress anyone because you have toxic plants in the cabinet. While it sounds very mysterious to work with old and gothic poisonous herbs, it's safest to leave toxic herbs alone when you are working herb magic. There are plenty of other safer and easy-to-acquire herbal materials available to you.

Herb Magic Terms You Should Know

The chief merit of language is clearness,
and we know that nothing detracts so much from this
as do unfamiliar terms.

—GALEN

As you begin to study herbal plants, don't let yourself be thrown by the technical jargon. Let's go over some of the terms and lingo you may encounter while studying herbs and herb magic. This may prevent you from making a mistake. If nothing else, think about how much smarter you'll feel the next time you thumb through any type of magical book featuring magical plants, trees, and herbs. Plus, the plant terminology does come in handy when you go to a nursery or garden center.

Amulet

A type of herbal charm, ornament, or jewel that aids and protects its wearer.

Annual

A plant that completes its life cycle in one growing season.

Baneful (Herb)

A toxic herb. A poisonous herb that causes death if ingested.

Biennial

A plant that grows vegetatively the first year and then is fruiting or dormant the second year. Foxglove, hollyhocks, mullein, and Queen Anne's lace are prime examples.

Chaplet

A wreath or garland of flowers and herbal foliage worn on the head. These chaplets traditionally symbolized victory or joy. They are popular adornments for Olympic athletes and, of course, brides. Today, they may be employed during ceremonies and special rituals, dedications, initiations, or handfastings, or at sabbat celebrations.

Charm

A rhyming series of words (a simple spell) used for a specific magical purpose.

Charm Bag

Similar to a sachet, a charm bag is a small cloth bag filled with aromatic herbs, charged crystals, and other magical ingredients. Charm bags may be carried for any magical purpose: health, safe travel, protection, to increase your confidence, and so on.

Cold Hardiness Zone

The cold hardiness zone is designed to help gardeners predict where a particular plant will thrive in a specific area. The plant hardiness zone map divides the United States and Canada into eleven zones, and is based on the average minimum winter temperature of an area.

Cultivar

A cultivar is a variant of a plant that has particular characteristics, such as leaf or flower variation. This new variant is developed and maintained under cultivation. The name of the cultivar is printed in roman type, within single quotation marks, and is capitalized. An example is this popular and hearty variety of lavender: *Lavandula* x *angustifiolia* 'Munstead.' Munstead is the name of the cultivar.

Cunning Man

An old term, traditionally meaning a male practitioner of magic and natural or holistic healing.

Deciduous

Trees, plants, and shrubs that shed their foliage in the fall and become dormant in the winter months.

Enchant

The classic definition is to "sing to." To enchant something means that you load or charge the object with your personal power and positive intentions.

Flower Fascination

"Fascination" is the art of directing another's consciousness or will toward you; to command or bewitch. Flower fascinations are elementary flower spells and floral charms used for various magical purposes.

Garden Witch

A practical, down-to-earth type of practitioner. A Witch who is well versed in herbal knowledge and its uses, and is a magical gardener.

Genus

A genus contains one species or several related species. The name appears in italic type and is designated by a Latin, capitalized singular noun, such as the genus for yarrow: *Achillea.*

Herbaceous Perennial

A plant that is nonwoody, and whose aboveground parts usually die back to the ground each winter. These plants survive by means of their vigorous root systems.

Herbalism

The use of herbs in conjunction with magic to bring about positive change.

Hybrid

A hybrid plant is created when two dissimilar plant species are crossed. Hybridized roses usually spring to mind, but mints, echinacea, columbine, and other herbs such as yarrow may be hybrids too. A hybrid is indicated by a multiplication sign, e.g., *Achillea* x *lewisii*. The specific cultivar name of this variety of blooming yarrow plant is 'King Edward.'

Perennial

A perennial plant is one that lives for three or more years.

Pocket Charm

A pocket charm is a tiny charm bag or herbal amulet that you can carry in your pocket while you are on the go.

Posy

An old term for a small, hand-held bouquet. Also known as a tussie-mussie or nosegay.

Sachet

A small cloth bag filled with aromatic herbs and spices.

Simple

A simple is a basic element; a charm or spell that features only one ingredient, such as an enchanted herb.

Simpling

The art of simpling consists of working with one select magical herb or flower. These spells and charms are quick and, well, *simple.*

Strewing Herbs

In medieval times, folks used to toss rushes and sweet-smelling herbs on the floors of their homes. This disguised bad smells and helped keep fleas and insects at bay. Some popular strewing herbs were meadowsweet, basil, lavender, and fennel. These aromatic herbs were "strewn" on the floor and thus came to be known as strewing herbs.

Tender perennial

A tender perennial is a plant that, while listed as a "perennial," will not likely survive the winter season unless steps are taken to protect it from the cold. Many varieties of basil, rosemary, and lavender are tender perennials.

Wisewomen

The first Witches and the custodians of the old herbal knowledge of benevolent spells and charms.

Wort Cunning

Herb craft. *Wort* is an old word for "herb."

Tools of the Trade

Every tool carries with it the spirit by which it has been created.

—WERNER KARL HEISENBERG

All lines of work have their own buzz words and special tools of the trade. Herb magic is no different. Now, while I'm not big on telling folks that they must have certain special accessories and doodads, there are a few things that come in handy when working herbal enchantments. If you don't have the following tools, don't run around in a panic. Take your time and enjoy hunting for them. If you can't find a mortar and pestle at ye old magic shop, then try a specialty spice shop or kitchen store.

You may already have a few of these accessories, like the scissors, which work well for snipping off herbal foliage. Actually, I usually use my garden scissors or pruning shears when I gather herbal materials. That way I get a good, clean cut. As for the fabric, check clearance tables at arts and crafts stores for sale pieces of plain, unbleached muslin or even celestial prints. Watch for spools of satin ribbon to go on sale. You can probably snag several for just a few dollars, and then you'll have some on hand for charm bags and herbal sachets. Also, there are really easy and inexpensive ways of creating a drying rack. So no worries—be creative. Look around and see what you have at home that you can work with.

Sickle

A sickle is a small hand-held knife with a blade shaped like a curving crescent. The shape of the blade mimics the moon and makes it a sacred tool for gathering herbs. If you have small hands, a sickle may be difficult to work with, so take your time and find a blade that feels comfortable to you.

Scissors

I have a sickle, but I prefer to use scissors. My gardens are large, and the chances of being outdoors during the day without a neighbor popping over to say hello are slim. It's hard to be discreet with a sickle, especially since mine has purple cords and beads hanging from it, so my garden scissors work out well.

Gathering Basket

A shallow and wide, flat-bottomed basket is ideal, but in a pinch, any type of wicker or wooden basket will do. I like a basket with a handle long enough that I can easily tuck my arm through it. That way my hands are free. With this style of basket, you can easily carry your shears, scissors, or sickle and still have rooms for herbal material.

Mortar and Pestle

This comes in handy for grinding up dried herbs and spices. The mortar is the cup, and the pestle is the grinder. The shapes of these tools are symbolic. The mortar, like the cup, is considered feminine, and the pestle is considered masculine. Take a look at the shapes of the pieces, and you'll get the idea. A mortar and pestle made from non-porous material is best to work with. A nonporous surface will not absorb any oils or scents from the ground-up herbs, so it will be easier to keep clean. In a pinch, you can use a blender or food processor to grind up your herbs. But please be safe, and make sure you wash it out thoroughly when you are finished. Before you cringe at the thought of using some modern appliance to work your herb magic, take a deep breath and relax. Sometimes you gotta go with what you've got.

Drying Rack

This is just what it sounds like: a rack to arrange herbs on so they can dry out without going moldy. This is actually pretty simple to make. One easy method is to staple pieces of cheesecloth over the top of a shallow, open cardboard box. Stretch the fabric tight. That way, the herbs lie on the taut, gauzy fabric, and air can circulate on all sides. You can also bind the herbs into small bundles and wrap each end with a rubber band. Then open one end of a paper clip, and hook it under the rubber band. Use the other end of the clip as a hanger, and hang the bundle upside down to dry.

Candles and Candle Holders

Yes, candles are tools utilized in herb magic. A burning spell candle is actually a physical symbol of your spell. So long as the candle burns, your spell is working. Plus, the element of fire is the element of transformation, so use this transformative power to your advantage. The following list of candle colors will help you link your herb magic together. Adding the enchantment of candles to your herb magic bumps up the volume of your spell. You can choose whatever type of candle you prefer, such as tapers, votives, mini spell candles, or tealights. By matching the color of the candle to your intention, you add the power of light, color, and fire to your herb magic. Be sure to burn your candles in a safe place and in the appropriate holder to avoid accidents. Here is a list of candle colors and their magical meanings.

Candle Colors and Magic

Pink—Affection, friendship, warm fuzzies, children's magic

Red—Love, passion, courage, the element of fire, the Mother Goddess

Orange—Energy, vitality, harvest, intensity

Yellow—Creativity, communication, knowledge, the element of air

Green—Prosperity, health, gardening, herbalism, faery magic, the earth element, the Green Man (God of Nature)

Blue—Peace, hope, healing, the element of water

Purple—Psychic powers, spirituality, to increase personal power, faery magic

Brown—Homes, pets, garden magic

Black—For protection, for breaking hexes, to banish illness and negativity, the Crone Goddess

White—All-purpose color, peace, calm, hope, the Maiden Goddess

Gray—Bindings, neutrality, invisibility spells and glamours

Silver—The Goddess, women's mysteries, the moon

Gold—The God, success, wealth, fame, the sun

Fabric and Ribbon

You'll want to have fabric and ribbon in various colors on hand for herbal sachets and charm bags. Also try working with those sheer-organza favor bags that have become so popular for bridal favors. They have a drawstring top, and the herbs are visible through the sheer and shimmery fabric. Refer to the previous candle color list to link the fabric color for your charm bag to the theme of your spell. Organza bags may be reused when you have finished with the sachet. Just return the contents to nature, and wash out the bag by hand. Allow the bag to air-dry, and it will be good to go for the next spell.

Glass Jars

A nice selection of bell jars is great for storing your magical herbs. You can always run old glass jelly jars or baby food jars through the dishwasher to sterilize them. These work nicely. I have also had good luck finding colored glass jars in funky shapes and sizes in kitchen specialty stores. These tinted jars have cork tops, and the colored glass protects your herbs from direct sunlight. Plus, I will admit the different shapes and sizes help me identify the herbs at a glance. For example, in my magical cabinet, the lavender buds are always in the short, square glass jar, while the dried bergamot heads are in a small eight-sided jar that reminds me of a salt shaker. As mentioned in the first chapter, be sure to keep these separate from your cooking herbs and spices.

Work Space

While this is not technically a tool, a space set aside to work your herb magic is a wonderful thing to have. Some practitioners move around. For example, I have cast herb magic all over my house and yard: at the kitchen counter, while sitting at a patio table in my gardens, and even while sitting on the grass, tucked under a shady tree. It all depends on how formal you wish to be. Perhaps you'd like to work at an altar specifically reserved for herb magic. Well, here are a few ideas for you to try out. Use the following suggestions as guidelines, and be creative.

Some magical folks use illuminator candles, which are often white tapers set up in attractive candle holders. These are placed in the back of the work space to provide illumination, hence the name, and they set a lovely mood. You can include a representation of the God and Goddess. Artwork is nice, or a simple and earthy option would be to include a fresh rose in a vase for the Goddess, and a few acorns or an oak leaf for the God. You may also want a cloth to cover the work area. This could be as simple as a scarf or a small tablecloth, or even a placemat. I have seen placemats with herbal patterns and themes that would be pretty sharp.

Again, go with what you prefer. You can make the setup simple or elaborate, according to your mood or personal taste. I also like to include representations of each of the four elements on my herb magic altars: a burning tealight in a holder for fire, a crystal point for earth, a feather for air, and a seashell for water. These items are small and can be grouped together and kept out of the way so you have more working space for your herbs and tools.

The Herbs, Planets, and Elements

As you read along in this book, you will notice that the featured herbs have astrological/planetary and elemental correspondences. These correspondences give character and direction to your herb magic. For example, the majority of the herbs listed in chapter 3, "Herb Magic for Love and Happiness," have the elemental association of water, and many have the planetary correspondence of Venus.

Why is this such a big deal? Because the planet Venus was named after the Roman goddess of love, Venus. So spells and charms cast on Friday—the day of the week with that planetary association—are perfect for working toward love and happiness. Take a look again at that "Days of the Week and Their Herb Magic Correspondences" section at the beginning of this chapter. All of the planetary associations and their symbols are right there for you to refer to.

The elemental correspondences of herbs add even more energies to the mix. Now, some folks don't pay any attention to herbal elemental associations, and quite frankly, you'll have to decide for yourself how complicated you'd like your spellcasting to be. The basic elemental data are provided here for you to consult, for your general information, so do with this information as you see fit. However, if we quickly break it down, the four natural elements bring specific vibrations and energies to their associated plants. The elements lend a certain *flavor* to their herbs, so to speak.

Earth—Prosperity, grounding, security, and stability

Air—Knowledge, wisdom, change, and intuition

Fire—Passion, energy, protection, and transformation

Water—Love, emotion, healing, and psychic powers

Without Further Ado . . .

Now that you understand the basics, it's time to move on to the spellcasting section of the book. Let's see . . . we went over how herb magic works, the rules of magic, and the elements of spellwork. We studied the simple planetary and herbal associations of the days of the week, and how to combine lunar timing and candle magic to your advantage.

You also have a good idea of the terms and the tools required for working herb magic. So guess where that leaves us? On to the good stuff—the spells.

The next four chapters will each focus on one of four specific topics: love and happiness, well-being and comfort, protection, and prosperity. Here, you'll find plant folklore and dozens of positive herbal spells and charms. These spells will incorporate other varieties of magic, such as color and candle magic, planetary symbols, and astrological timing (which we have already discussed). See, there *is* a method to my madness.

So without further ado, let's get to it!

A loving heart is the truest wisdom.

—CHARLES DICKENS

CHAPTER THREE

HERB MAGIC FOR LOVE AND HAPPINESS

As we begin these specialty chapters, you will notice that they are all set up in a similar fashion. Each chapter begins with a "Spells from the Spice Rack" section, so all of those culinary herbs in your kitchen can be put to practical use. I did not want to overlook these seasonings, as many of you will already have them at home. Then there is a segment featuring plants that you may not know are herbs. Next is a section on the enchantment of herbal trees, and finally, a bit of garden witchery. By "garden witchery," I mean working with herbal plants commonly grown in the garden— from the garden straight into the cauldron, as it were.

In each of these specialty chapters, you will find the planetary and elemental correspondences for the featured herbs, a touch of herbal legend, and an accompanying herbal spell. You will also discover the most opportune day and/or moon phase for your herb magic. All four chapters are crammed full of herbal information, fun folklore, practical magic, and quick and easy spells and charms.

For spells that revolve around love and happiness, try working on a Friday, the day of the week that is dedicated to the Norse goddess of love, Freya. The planetary correspondence for Friday is the planet Venus, as we discussed in the previous chapter. Once again, the astrological symbol for Venus is ♀. You could also work on a Tuesday, the day dedicated to the Roman god Mars, to add some fiery passion to the mix. The astrological symbol for Mars is ♂. Yes, I'm sure you've noticed that these are also the symbols for female and male. You could incorporate either of these symbols into your herb magic by carving it into a candle, or drawing or stitching it onto a charm bag or sachet. Use your imagination, and see what you can conjure up.

So settle in and get ready to learn some practical tips and tricks. We'll have some fun, expand your knowledge of the topic, and learn all about the wonderful world of herb magic.

Loving Spells from the Spice Rack

It is a fine seasoning for joy to think of those we love.

—MOLIÈRE

Basil

Basil *(Ocimum basilicum)* is an annual herb that corresponds to the planet Mars and the element of fire. It is a native of India and is sacred to the Hindu god Vishnu. According to European herbal folklore, basil created sympathy between people and promoted love. Easy to grow in most sunny gardens, basil is wonderful to have on hand to add to culinary dishes.

The licorice scent of fresh basil encourages loving feelings between two people, which may explain the old herbal folklore that if a man accepts a basil plant from a woman, he will love her forever afterward. You may add dried basil leaves to spells and charms designed to keep your lover faithful to you. Plus, sprinkling dried basil leaves around the bedroom will banish any negative emotions and bad feelings after a lover's spat. In herb magic, basil is used to purify sacred spaces. Try this quick herbal charm and see how it works out for you.

The Lover's Spat Spell

For best results, try working this herbal spell on a Friday, the day of the week that's filled with romantic and loving energies. If you'd like to add lunar energies to this spell, work during the full moon, for power, or the waning moon, to banish negativity. To begin, sprinkle a pinch of dried basil leaves in each of the four corners of your bedroom, working in a clockwise direction. Repeat the charm softly as you go around the room:

Around the bedroom I sprinkle these fragrant leaves,
Now, banish anger and negativity please.
Clear the air and smooth over this lover's spat.
Happiness does prevail, our love will stand fast.

Chili Pepper

Chili pepper *(Capsicum* ssp.), also known as red pepper, is a popular cooking herb found in the spice racks of most homes. The chili corresponds to the planet Mars and the element of fire. Capsicums were first brought to Europe from Mexico after Columbus's travels. These plants are annuals and grow into small bushy plants, bearing their fruits in the summer months. In your herb magic, you may use either the dried pepper flakes or the whole chili, whichever you prefer.

When handling whole chilies, please be sure to keep your hands away from your face, especially your eyes. Hot chili peppers can cause skin irritation and make your eyes burn badly. I have found old herbal spells that call for tying together two chili peppers with a scarlet ribbon and tucking them beneath your pillow to keep your lover faithful—not a good idea. Instead, I'd tuck the peppers under the bed (as long as your pets won't nibble on them) or hang the ribbon-bound chilies in the bedroom, but well away from the bed.

For a safer alternative, try working with dried red pepper flakes. Add red pepper flakes to passion-enhancing sachets and charms, or sprinkle a bit onto an unlit spell candle to bring some passion back to your love life. Try this next spicy candle spell and see if you can add a little *heat* to your love life. *Muy caliente!*

Spicy Candle Spell

This spell is intended for couples who have a dedicated relationship. It isn't for a one-night stand sort of deal. You may customize this spell by adding your wedding photo, or a happy photo of the two of you. Other options include writing your and your partner's names on a small piece of paper that you can slip under the candle holder. If you take a look at the closing lines of the spell, you will see that it includes a rider. You should keep this spell affectionate, and get your partner's permission *before* you go and put an herbal passion whammy on him or her. Casting magic on another without permission is manipulation, and the spell will probably backfire if you aren't working conscientious magic. If you need to, go back and review the section "The Basic Rules of Magic" in chapter 1.

You may work this spell on a Friday, Venus's day, or even a Tuesday, for passion and extra energy. A coordinating lunar phase would be during the waxing moon. Casting a romance spell during a waxing moon will pull things toward you. As the moon increases, so does the loving energy of the magic.

Set up your work space as you desire, and then sprinkle a pinch of red pepper flakes onto an unlit small red candle (any style you prefer—taper, mini spell candle, or votive) or in the bottom of the cup of a white tealight candle. Put the tealight back in its cup, or slip the red candle in a holder. Wash and dry your hands. Then light the candle and repeat this charm three times:

> *Flames of love burn, with spicy red pepper,*
> *Boost desire and bring us together.*
> *Now bring some passion back between us two,*
> *An enchanted evening for me and you.*
> *By all the powers of the moon and sun,*
> *For the good of all, bringing harm to none.*

Allow the candle to burn in a safe place until it is consumed.

Marjoram

Marjoram *(Origanum majorana)* comes in many varieties and may be an annual, biennial, or perennial plant. This is a versatile and popular cooking herb, with a sweet and spicy taste. Marjoram was cultivated in medieval times for its fragrance, to attract bees. It was also valued as a strewing herb, and was added to potpourris and perfumes. Marjoram has the planetary correspondence of Mercury and is aligned with the element of air.

This fragrant herb has links in folklore to the goddess Aphrodite, who created it as a symbol of happiness. Marjoram was thought to have grown in Aphrodite's garden on

Mount Olympus, and it's believed that the goddess herself blessed the plant with its charming scent. A popular folk name for marjoram is "joy of the mountain," perhaps for the joy it brought to the Goddess in her garden. In olden times, chaplets and garlands were made from marjoram for blessing brides and grooms. Marjoram is often worked into spells that encourage long-term love, as its energies are harmonious with enduring relationships. Its scent is thought to bestow happiness and a sweet, restful sleep.

Herbal Sachet for Happy and Loving Dreams

As discussed in chapter 2, a sachet is a scented herbal charm bag. Here is a recipe and spell for a charming herbal sachet.

To begin, purchase a small, sheer, pink favor bag. (These organza bags are very popular as wedding favors and may be found in arts and crafts stores in the bridal section.) Or sew your own out of plain pink or white fabric, and tie it closed with pink ribbons.

Work this spell on a Friday, during a waxing or full moon. The herbal components of this spell—marjoram, rose petals, and violets—were sacred to the goddess Aphrodite and will work in harmony with each other.

To the sachet bag add fresh or dried marjoram leaves, and violet flowers or foliage. These can often be found growing in your yard. Add fresh pink rose petals to the mixture, and tie the bag closed. Next, hold the sachet in both hands, and visualize it surrounded by a warm pink light. Repeat the following verse three times:

> *Marjoram leaves tucked in a sweet-smelling sachet,*
> *Will chase away the blues and keep bad dreams away.*
> *Add violets for the Lady, and the rose for love,*
> *Aphrodite, hear my call, and answer from above.*

Tuck the sachet under your pillow, or place it on your nightstand. As you get ready for bed, close the spell with these lines:

> *Pink sachet bag and enchanted herbs so sweet,*
> *Bring to me loving, sweet dreams and restful sleep.*

Thyme

Thyme *(Thymus vulgaris)* is a multibranching, low plant with woody stems and plentiful small, pointed, and strongly scented leaves. This shrubby, fragrant plant is a native of the Mediterranean regions. This lovely herb corresponds with the planet Venus and the element of water. This ties in neatly to this chapter's theme, as both Venus and the element of water are associated with love. Thyme has long been associated with Witchcraft and magic, and is listed as one of the nine Anglo-Saxon magical herbs. There are over 300 varieties of thyme, and it is a popular culinary herb used to flavor poultry, soups, and stews.

According to herbal folklore, wearing a sprig of flowering thyme in your hair is believed to make you irresistible to the opposite sex. Plus, it is thought to grant you the ability to see the elves and the faeries. To the Greeks this was a symbol of courage, and the Romans believed that it was a remedy for melancholy.

This plant will attract many bees, and blossoming thyme and bees were popular themes for ladies embroidery in medieval times. It was common for this herb to be embroidered on a lady's scarf and then presented as a favor to her knight. I would imagine this was a quiet way to give the bearer's courage a magical boost, and to symbolize his lady's affections.

Thyme was, and still is today, planted into a low herbal hedge for knot gardens. It was also planted together with lavender to help both plants grow stronger. This is often referred to these days as companion planting.

An old herbal spell calls for a maiden to place a sprig of thyme in one of her shoes and a sprig of rosemary in the other. The maiden was to sprinkle her shoes with water three times and place them alongside her bed. Then she said a prayer and turned in for the night, and was to expect a vision of her future husband. The original spell was to be performed on the night of January 20, on St. Agnes' Eve. Nowadays, I'd try this herb spell on the night of a full moon.

All in Good Thyme: A Divination Spell

Work this enchantment during the full moon. For this spell you will need a pair of your shoes, a few tablespoons of water, a sprig of thyme, and a sprig of rosemary. (If you can't get your hands on the fresh herbs, use a pinch of dried thyme and dried rosemary.) Tuck the thyme in your right shoe and the rosemary in your left. Then confidently set the shoes in your bedroom in a place where the light of the full moon will shine down on them. Sprinkle three drops of water on the shoes and herbs (just a bit of water—you don't want to ruin your shoes), and then just before you turn in for the night, repeat this charm three times:

In the light of the moon, I work this old herbal spell,
By my will and desire, may it all turn out well.
A vision of my future love, reveal to me this night,
A dream conjured from rosemary, thyme,
and silver moonlight.

In the morning, write down any dreams you had. Return the herbs to nature, and keep your eyes open until the next full moon to see what, or who, turns up.

Vanilla

Vanilla *(Vanilla planifolia)* is one of the most popular flavorings in the world and can be found in almost everybody's spice rack. This herb is also associated with the loving energies of the planet Venus and the element of water. The scent and taste of vanilla are thought to be aphrodisiacs. The vanilla bean is valued as a flavoring in puddings, sauces, cakes, candies, and liqueurs. Vanilla beans are grown in Madagascar, Mexico, Indonesia, and Tahiti. Vanilla originated in Mexico, where the Aztecs used it to enhance the flavor of their chocolate drinks. The Mexican Emperor Montezuma introduced vanilla to Cortez, who then brought it to Europe in the sixteenth century.

The long, yellow-green seed pods of this tropical orchid plant are gathered before the plant flowers. The pods are picked when they are unripe (green) and then cured slowly over a period of six months until they are brown. To obtain pure vanilla extract, the cured vanilla beans are steeped in alcohol. According to law, pure vanilla extract must be 35 percent alcohol by volume.

This herb is easiest to work with in its extract or essential oil form; however vanilla beans are not that expensive and are fun to use. Try a specialty cooking store or a spice shop to find the beans. A vanilla bean may be added to a love sachet or tucked in your pocket to boost your aura and increase your attraction to another. Carrying vanilla beans adds sort of a "Hey, I'm one irresistible and fascinating person!" vibe to your personality. According to herbal folklore, men find the scent of vanilla to be sexually arousing. Now you know why, in the old days, women would dab a little vanilla extract behind their ears.

Vanilla Bean Spell: A Pocket Charm

A pocket charm is just what it sounds like: a little talisman or herbal amulet that you can tuck in your pocket and take with you. This pocket charm will help draw loving vibrations and a fun relationship toward you. This could be a romance, or it might be a wonderful friendship. Don't try to direct the energy of this charm too much—just enjoy the ride and see what happens!

Work this spell on a Venus day (Friday) and during a waxing moon. For this pocket charm you will need:

- 1 vanilla bean
- A 4-inch square of plain fabric
- A permanent marker (your choice of color), which you will use to draw the astrological symbol for Venus (♀) and a heart on the fabric
- 12 inches of red or pink (whichever color you prefer) satin ribbon

Place the vanilla bean in the center of the fabric square. If the bean is long, you can gently fold it in half so it will stay within the fabric. Gather up each of the four corners of the fabric, one by one, repeating a line of the following charm at each corner:

By the earth, I consecrate this loving pocket charm.
By air, I cast out all negativity and harm.
By fire, I add the warmth and passion of love.
By water, I bless this charm that herb magic wove.

Now bind the pocket charm with the ribbon. Tie a bow and knot it securely closed. Close the charm with these lines:

For the good of all, bringing harm to none,
May this herbal spell bring affection and fun.

Romantic Plants You May Not Know Are Herbs

The red rose whispers of passion,
And the white rose breathes of love;
O, the red rose is a falcon,
And the white rose is a dove.

—JOHN BOYLE O'REILLY

Yes, this section is dedicated to plants you may not know are also classified as herbs. The following romantic plants are all considered herbs. Remember that to be classified as an herb, some part of the plant (the leaves, flowers, fruits, or roots) must be used for food, medicine, flavoring, or scent.

Rose

Roses *(Rosa)* are also associated with the planet Venus and the element of water. Just as you'd expect, this flower is sacred to some of our more popular love goddesses, such as Aphrodite, Venus, and Freya. These gorgeous flowers come in dozens of colors and forms, and the different colors of roses all have different magical meanings. Roses have been cultivated for thousands of years. The Apothecary's rose, one of the oldest varieties of garden roses, was widely grown in medieval times for its medicinal properties. Once upon a time, roses were highly valued for their medicinal properties (the hips are high in vitamin C), and utilized for culinary purposes as well as for their fragrance.

Rose buds and petals are classic ingredients in love spells, plus the plants attract the faeries when grown in your garden. Magically, you can add rose petals to spells when you want to "speed things up." Also, the fruits of the rose (the hips) may be strung together onto a thin red ribbon or string with a large, sharp needle. These herbal "beads" are then worn to attract love and companionship. Plus, those dried rose hips are great to add to healing and happiness spells and to put into charm bags that will help make the recipient feel loved and cared for.

The rose has the enchanting ability to teach you how to enjoy giving of yourself, your time and talents, to help others. This flower symbolizes the greatest characteristics of the Goddess: the capacity to love and nurture, and to see beauty in everything.

You can use the following list of rose colors and their magical meanings as a quick reference guide when designing your own herbal spells. You can work with a fresh rose in a vase of water, or you can gently strip the petals and add them to charm bags and sachets. Those fragrant petals are also lovely sprinkled across your altar, or you can use them to cast a physical circle on the ground. Remember, if you can't grow roses at home, you can always pop into a floral shop and pick up a stem or two.

Rose Colors and Magic

Burgundy—Symbolizes a deeper, darker, more tempestuous love

Celadon Green—Symbolizes prosperity, fertility, and good luck; celadon is a pale to very pale green, a very chic color for roses these days

Coral—Charm and affection

Hot Pink—Announces passion, daring, and verve

Ivory—Romance and a steadfast, mature love

Orange—Vitality, passion, and energy

Pale Pink—Pastel-pink roses symbolize romance and a dreamy first love; use this color to invoke a warm, fuzzy feeling

Purple—Power, passion, and the enchantment of the faeries

Red—True love, lust, and romance

Red and White—Creativity, unity, and solidarity

Yellow—Joy and happiness, communication, and the power of the sun

White—Peace, love, moon magic, new beginning

All-Purpose Herbalist's Spell

Here is an all-purpose spell for your herb magic. It calls upon the historical knowledge of the wisewomen and the cunning men, the first true "wise ones." This herb magic also taps into your own inner wisdom and power. The following spell will work nicely with rose color magic or for other positive spells that you will soon be conjuring up on your own. Happy casting!

> *May the wise ones of old hear me in this hour,*
> *As I call on the herbalist's inner power.*
> *By color and scent, this herbal spell is begun,*
> *As I will so mote it be, an let it harm none.*

Chapter Three

Wild Strawberry

The strawberry *(Fragaria vesca)* is a plant native to North America and Britain. It was known to the ancient Britons, Romans, and Anglo-Saxons. This plant, like many others in this chapter, corresponds to the planet Venus and the element of water. The strawberry is sacred to the Norse goddess of love, Freya, and this fruit has many ties to sexuality and love. Traditionally, strawberries were used in medieval literature and art as a representation of desire and mortal love. On the opposite side of the leaf, the strawberry was also a symbol of perfection and virtue.

The fresh fruit of the strawberry was once crushed and used to lighten freckles, soothe sunburn, and help whiten stained teeth. As you would imagine, strawberries are eaten raw, added to desserts and to flavor liqueurs and cordials, and, of course, cooked into preserves, jams, and jellies. The strawberry's leaves are used as a relaxing tea and as a wash for oily skin. The dried leaves are also added to potpourri for their texture and scent.

Strawberries are a food of love—think chocolate-covered strawberries for Valentine's Day, or imagine feeding your love fresh strawberries dipped in cream. Also, the leaves of the wild strawberry may be worked into a sachet or herbal charm to help safeguard a pregnancy.

A Scented Strawberry Spell to Remove Sour Vibes

For this subtle herbal spell, we are going to incorporate a touch of magical aromatherapy. This spell comes in handy for those times when you've had a spat with your love. We all have really silly arguments and bicker with each other from time to time. So, if you need to clear the air and get rid of any hard feelings still hanging around, this is just the ticket.

Take a look around and see if you can find a red, strawberry-scented votive candle and strawberry-scented incense. You will also need some fresh strawberries, so pop into the grocery store and purchase a small container. If you have access to wild strawberry foliage growing in your yard, you may add this to the spell.

Note: If you are allergic to strawberries, try using fresh raspberries or blackberries instead.

A Friday would be wonderful for this herb magic. Why? Well, it is the day associated with the goddess Freya. Strawberries are sacred to Freya, and this is the day of the week that takes its name from this Norse goddess of love—Freya's Day. Work this spell during the *waning* moon, if possible. (See, not every spell in this chapter calls for a waxing moon.) We need to work in a waning moon this time because we want to send the sour feelings on their way and to decrease those hurt feelings. As the moon gets smaller in the sky, so will those hurt feelings diminish.

Set the votive candle in a candle cup, or set the incense in its holder. Arrange the fruit and the foliage (if you choose to use it) in a circle around the candle or incense. Be sure to keep the foliage well away from any open flame. Now light the candle/incense and wait a few moments until the scent begins to waft around the room. While you are waiting for the scent to be released, take a moment to see if you can come up with a few apologies or, conversely, a few ways to accept an apology graciously.

> *Freya, goddess of love, hear my plea,*
> *Help end the tiff between my love and me.*
> *By color and scent, this berry spell begins.*
> *With love and affection this charm will spin.*

Choose one berry and taste it. Feel the sweet and tart taste explode in your mouth. Remember that every relationship requires hard work, and does have its ups and downs. Life is not a romance novel, so don't hang on to anger over trivial things. The world's not going to end because you had a spat. Take a deep breath, and ground and center, releasing your anger and hurt feelings. Now, finish the berry and close the spell with these lines:

> *Freya, I do thank you for your time and care.*
> *I close this spell by earth, water, flame, and air.*

Sweet Violet

The perennial violet *(Viola odorata)* has pretty, heart-shaped leaves and thrives in shady places from winter to spring. The violet is, as many of the featured plants in this chapter, aligned with the planet Venus and the element of water. This little flower is sacred to Aphrodite/Venus, as are the majority of blue flowers. Occasionally, you may find white violets growing wild in the backyard or woods. If you do, leave them as they are. Treasure these charming flowers for the magical gifts they are. Legend states that they are faery plants, and to pick them is to anger the faery realm.

Violets were held in high regard in ancient times. The flower has an subtle scent and has become the symbol for constancy. Violet flowers can be washed gently, coated with sugar, and then frozen or simply patted dry and added to salads. Many old herbals list dozens of medicinal uses for the violet, but here I'd like to focus on the magical ones.

Wearing a chaplet or wreath of violets in your hair offers a strong magical protection and, according to herbal folklore, cures a headache. Also, wearing a chaplet of violets is a charm against being faery-led—in other words, having the faeries confuse you or becoming lost. Old herbal spells often call for mixing violets and lavender together in a potent herbal sachet to arouse love and desire. Hmmm . . . Sounds like a good way to spice things up with your partner! Let's put a modern spin on this and see what we come up with.

Violet and Lavender Sachet for Desire

Create this charm bag during a waxing moon. Work on a Friday, for love, or a Tuesday, to increase passion. Use a sheer pink favor bag, or make your own with plain pink fabric and pink ribbons. If you don't want to work with pink fabrics, try a dark purple for passion and power. Or how about red for lust and love? It's up to you. Don't be bashful about putting your own spin on things!

Fill the bag with a half cup of dried lavender buds, and tuck in six fresh, tiny violet blossoms. (If wild violets are out of season, you may substitute these with a few blossoms from a blooming African violet house plant.) Then knot the bag closed and charge the sachet with your positive intentions. Hold the sachet bag in your hands, and repeat the following spell three times:

> *With lavender buds and sweet violet blooms,*
> *Aphrodite, please hear this Witch's tune.*
> *Now stir up some passion, and heighten desire,*
> *And merrily off to bed we'll soon retire.*

Take the sachet bag and tuck it under your bed, hang it from the headboard, or set it neatly on your nightstand. At the risk of sounding like a mom, don't forget to practice safe sex while setting the stage for this enchanted evening! Close the spell with these lines:

> *For the good of all, bringing harm to no one,*
> *May this herbal spell bring passion and fun.*

Herbal Trees for Love

I am a willow of the wilderness,
Loving the wind that bent me.

—RALPH WALDO EMERSON

White Willow

This tree *(Salix alba)* corresponds with the moon and the element of water. This elemental association makes perfect sense, as willows typically like growing near the water. The willow tree may reach up to eighty feet in height, and the bark of the white willow has been utilized for centuries for its fever-reducing and pain-relieving properties. There are several Greek deities associated with the willow tree, including Artemis, Ceres, Hecate, Hera, Mercury, Persephone, and also the Greek sorceress Circe, who was a priestess of Hecate.

Willow leaves and twigs are often worked into love-promoting charms and spells. A small branch of willow would make a wonderful wand for use in any moon magic and, of course, for love spells. According to herbal folklore, artists, mystics, poets, and other wise folks would sit and meditate, write, or draw under the draping branches of the willow tree to revitalize themselves and to help gain a touch of divine inspiration.

Feeling down in the dumps, or a little blue? Sometimes the best thing we can do is to work for a loving relationship with *ourselves*. After all, if you are miserable with yourself, it's pretty tough to attract anything or anyone positive to you. Why not work with the power of the willow and bless yourself with a little happiness and self-love? Here is an old, reliable Witch's spell that is also a fun type of magic to perform with a group.

Willow Knot Spell

To have your spell wish granted, you are to stand under the graceful branches of the willow on the night of a full moon.

Blow a kiss to the moon and state your wish out loud, as you gently tie a loose knot in one of the supple branches. Then, while gazing up at the rising moon, repeat this verse:

> *Under the Lady's moon, shining so bright,*
> *Willow tree, hear my request on this night.*
> *In this willow tree, I now leave a marker,*
> *Grant me love and happiness, and bring much laughter.*

Close the spell with these standard Craft lines:

> *By all the power of three times three,*
> *And as I will it, so mote it be.*

Sugar Maple

The sugar maple *(Acer saccharum)* is also an herbal tree. It is associated with the planet Jupiter and the element of air. The sugar maple tree is famous for its leaves' gorgeous autumn colors and, naturally, the sap that is boiled and reduced into delicious maple syrup. When it comes to magic, the leaves of the maple tree can be added to any charm or spell when you need to "sweeten up" a situation or even another person. Now, before you start wondering about manipulation, hear me out.

We all have to deal with unpleasant co-workers, neighbors, in-laws, relatives, and other people. Adding maple leaves to your herbal charms only improves things, by smoothing over bad feelings. It gently fine-tunes a few cranky attitudes, but it doesn't radically change the other person. It only takes the edge off that person's nastiness.

So what this means is you have to put forth some *effort,* too. You will need to be considerate and kind to the person as well. As with many other things, you'll get out of this herbal charm what you are willing to put into it.

A Quick Maple Leaf Charm

This quick charm may be cast during a waxing moon, to attract more kindness and compassion into your life. Or in a pinch, you could work this during a waning moon, to help remove and dissipate those hard feelings. The only supplies you need are a few fallen maple leaves and your intentions.

Go outside at sunset, and gather up a handful of maple leaves. Silently turn and face the western direction. This quarter is associated with emotions and love, so we'd like to tap in to that. Now close your eyes and visualize the problematic person. Visualize all the negativity and stress you've built up worrying about the situation draining away and back into the earth. Gently, close your hands around the leaves, and empower them with your good will. Call the person by name and say out loud:

As I stand under a sunset sky,
There is now peace between you and I.

Cast the leaves to the breeze, and let them float to the ground. Now turn and walk confidently home.

Garden Witchery: From Garden to Cauldron

*There's rosemary and rue; these keep
Seeming and savor all the winter long.
Grace and remembrance be to you.*

—SHAKESPEARE, *A WINTER'S TALE*

Rosemary

Rosemary *(Rosmarinus officinalis)* is classified as a tender perennial, and has the planetary association of the Sun and the elemental correspondence of fire. Rosemary grows in the spring as a small, dense evergreen shrub with soft needlelike leaves and tiny blue flowers. This fragrant herb is a fabulous fresh ingredient for cooking—especially with soups, vegetables, venison, pork, and poultry. Rosemary comes in many enchanting varieties, but keep in mind that it will not survive harsh, cold winters.

If a rosemary plant has winter protection, it *might* have a chance. I have a huge rosemary plant in an unprotected area of my herb garden that, to my amazement, has managed to survive three midwestern winters so far. I mulch around the base with fallen leaves and leave it alone. I always wonder if it will survive the next year's snow and ice. This will be year four, and only time will tell.

Rosemary is one of my favorite Witchy herbs, and has a wonderful piny fragrance. Rosemary was a favored herb of the ancient Greeks and Romans. Because of its coastal growth habitat, it picked up the folk name "dew of the sea." It's rumored that the Greeks wore garlands of rosemary around their heads to help improve their memory. Also, since this herb symbolized remembrance, it was often incorporated into the flowers and herbs used at funerals.

In the old days, rosemary was popularly utilized as a decoration in weddings. The bride wove fresh sprigs into her chaplet, or tucked the green stems into her bouquet. The groom also wore a sprig of rosemary, in sort of an early version of the boutonnière. Also, it was traditional to hand out sprigs of the herb to the wedding guests. Herbal folk-lore tells us to tie the stems of these herbal wedding favors with a golden ribbon.

A modern option would be to place small potted plants of rosemary on the reception tables. Tie on a gold bow for decoration, and leave a note telling your guests the folklore of the herb and that they should take a plant home with them. This way, all who attended the wedding will be blessed with the vitality of this herb of the sun, and will be granted sweet memories of the couple's special day.

Rosemary Spell for a Wedding Day to Remember

If you'd like to try this herbal blessing for your wedding reception, gather all your pots of rosemary together before placing them on the tables. Hold your hands over the plants, and quietly repeat this charm three times:

> *The charming rosemary has a fragrant bouquet.*
> *Bring joy and sweet memories to our special day.*

Columbine

The columbine *(Aquilegia vulgaris)*, like so many other herbs in this chapter, is associated with the planet Venus and the element of water. This shady garden perennial is simple to grow and will hybridize easily with other colors and varieties of columbines. I planted a yellow and red columbine next to a purple one in my garden, and the new color variations they have produced are wonderful.

Historically, columbine carries the reputation of attracting love. Some antique herbal spells call for carrying the seeds on your person to achieve this result. I strongly advise against working with the seeds of the columbine, as they are toxic. The seeds contain hydrocyanic acid, and could have dire consequences if ingested by a child. Let's just avoid the whole problem; for safety's sake, I suggest working with the lovely multicolored blossoms instead.

Interestingly, this flower is associated with several birds. The botanical name for columbine, *Aquilegia*, is taken from the Latin word for *eagle*. This is due to the "spurs" of the flowers that somewhat resemble the talons of an eagle. An old Anglo-Saxon name for columbine is *culverwort*, which translates to "pigeon plant." Other plant folklore links this flowering herb to the dove, which was a sacred bird to the Greco-Roman goddess of love, Aphrodite/Venus.

Wings of a Dove: A Columbine Spell for Romance

If you'd like to bring a touch of herbal romance into your life, try working with the columbine blossoms. Refer to the list of colors in the section "Candle Colors and Magic" on pages 39–40, and match the color of the blossoms to your intent. Arrange the blossoms in a small vase, and set them in a place of prominence where you are sure to see them every day. Or, just leave the plants growing in the garden and work with them right where they are.

> *Columbine, colorful flower of love,*
> *Speed my request on the wings of a dove.*
> *Send to me romance, and one who will love me best.*
> *May the goddess of love smile upon my request.*

If you worked with columbine flowers in a vase, keep them until they start to fade. Then return them neatly to nature by adding them to a compost pile.

Yarrow

Yarrow *(Achillea millefolium)* is a beloved Witches' garden plant. Yarrow, too, is associated with the planet Venus and the element of water. This perennial is easy to find at local garden centers or nurseries and will do well in most sunny beds. Try some this year in your garden! Yarrow has historically been used in many of the wise folks' spells and charms. This is an herb that has links to the great Mother Goddess, and symbolizes maternal love.

Carrying yarrow blossoms in your pocket will attract a new love to you. Yarrow is often worked into love divinations. It has a reputation for keeping a married couple happily together for seven years, which earned it the folk name "seven years' love." Smelling the fragrance of yarrow blossoms is supposed to alleviate fears, remove glamours, and allow you to see events and situations more clearly.

Please note: If you have sensitive skin, wear gloves while handling this plant, as yarrow can cause contact dermatitis (a mild rash). Yarrow, if taken internally, can make the skin sensitive to sunlight. Yarrow should be avoided by pregnant and nursing women.

Historically, yarrow was rumored to stop a nosebleed, and was in addition called "wound wort." The plant takes its Latin name from Achilles, who was said to have learned about its medicinal uses from the centaur Chiron. Achilles was thought to have used this herb to dress his soldiers' wounds during the Trojan War.

There are lots of varieties and colors of yarrow, including one of my favorite cultivars, 'Moonshine.' This is a gorgeous and sturdy blooming herb with flat, golden-yellow flowers that hold their shape and color for a long time in the perennial garden. Once the flower has finished its bloom cycle, you can deadhead the plant and it will reward you with another, smaller bloom cycle in the fall.

Yarrow is a favorite blooming herb for women, Witches, and magical herbalists due to its easy growing habits and long-lasting blossoms, and the fact that its blossoms are all-purpose herbal flowers. The easy-to-dry flowers hold their color well and can be worked into lots of arts and crafts projects, or they can be stored neatly in a sealed jar for future spellwork.

If you'd like to begin planting a magical garden, perennial yarrow should be at the top of your list. Find a nice, sunny spot and work some organic compost well into your soil, to improve the nutrient level. It is important to work this soil amendment down into your existing soil—don't just dump it on top of the garden. Once you've worked it in and raked the area smooth, then arrange your yarrow in a place of prominence. When you have all the planting done, you may bless your plants and your enchanted garden with the following lines.

Garden Blessing Charm

Lovely yarrow is known as the wise woman's herb,
Elements four, gather 'round at the sound of my words.
Bless this garden with growth, health, and bounty, I pray,
Bringing wisdom, magic, and joy, day after day.

Need some more ideas for plotting out your own magical garden? For additional easy and practical gardening suggestions, flower folklore, and information about magical theme gardens—including plant suggestions for sun and shade, and enchanted garden layouts and plans—refer to my previous book *Garden Witchery*.

There is a comfort in the strength of love . . .
—WILLIAM WORDSWORTH

CHAPTER FOUR

HERB MAGIC FOR WELL-BEING AND COMFORT

Herb magic to promote well-being and comfort is probably one of the oldest forms of herbal uses. This, after all, was traditionally one of the main requests that an herbalist, wisewoman, or cunning man faced. As stated before, the following information is meant to be used magically. Do not attempt to "doctor" yourself with herbal remedies. Always seek the care of a physician, counselor, or licensed and qualified herbalist for any health problem or serious condition.

The spells in this chapter are designed to bring comfort, chase away the blues, increase personal energy, and encourage happiness. Always remember to get the recipient's permission first, no matter how good your intentions are. Without it, you are manipulating. Be sure to work for the good of all, bringing harm to none.

There is something so quietly satisfying about helping others. And there are plenty of magical things you *can* safely do—without manipulation—whether it's providing a sounding board, a sympathetic ear, or a shoulder to lean on. If you decide to add a touch of herb magic to your work, and the recipient is open to the idea, this chapter will give you plenty of ideas for herbal enchantments, with many different planetary associations and energies to try.

Comforting Spells from the Spice Rack

This must my comfort be,
The sun that warms you here shall shine upon me.

—SHAKESPEARE

Coriander

Coriander *(Coriandrum sativum)* has the planetary correspondence of Mars and the elemental association of fire. Coriander has been cultivated for the last 3,000 years or so. It's interesting to note that coriander seeds have been found in Egyptian tombs from the 21st Dynasty. The seeds were included in the tombs because they were thought to protect the soul of the deceased. Interestingly enough, most old herbals call for using the seeds in charms and spells. The Greeks and Romans were familiar with this herb, and many medieval herbals had various opinions on what this herb was to be used for—anything from healing open sores, to keeping vapors away from the head (whatever that means), to curing nosebleeds, to mixing it with violets to cure a hangover.

An old herbal charm for coriander instructed a woman who wished to conceive to strap thirteen coriander seeds to her left thigh, while Chinese herbalists believed that this herb granted immortality. Coriander seeds work well in herbal sachets and in potpourri, and may be tucked into charm bags or carried on a person to help alleviate headaches.

This fresh annual herb has a pungent scent and a strong taste, and the fresh green foliage of the plant is also known as cilantro. Today, coriander/cilantro is commonly used to flavor spicy Mexican foods, and is easy to find at the market with the other fresh herbs. Some folks dislike the scent of fresh cilantro. So, you may want to give the fresh leaves a careful sniff, to make sure you care for the aroma, before you try this next herbal spell.

Fresh green coriander/cilantro may be gathered together, bound with ribbon, and hung in the home to promote safety and to bestow peace on the occupants of the home.

Coriander Spell for Comfort and Peace

Work this enchantment on a Thursday, for healing, or a Sunday, for happiness and success. If you feel that there are a lot of bad vibes hanging around and you want to go all out, cast on a Saturday, to banish any negativity in the home.

Gather together a small bundle of the fresh herb, and bind it together with a satin ribbon. The choice of color for the ribbon is up to you. You could go with red for protection, blue to bring peace, or even green for healing. Be sure to personalize this herbal spell to suit your needs. Once you've tied it up, hang the herb bundle in a prominent spot (I'd suggest the kitchen) and allow it to dry out. Repeat this spell as you hang the herbs:

> *Coriander or cilantro, call it what you will,*
> *Display this herb in the home, and add a little thrill.*
> *Promote protection and safety to this house, we pray,*
> *Bringing comfort, happiness, and peace, both night and day.*

Nutmeg

Nutmeg *(Myristica fragrans)* is associated with the planet Jupiter and the element of fire. Nutmeg and mace are typical spice-rack favorites. What I find interesting about them is that they are actually different parts of the same fruit of the evergreen nutmeg tree.

The fruit splits open into a red outer membrane (mace) and an inner brown seed (nutmeg). Even though they come from the same fruit, nutmeg has a stronger aroma and tastes sweeter than mace. The plant is native to Indonesia, Brazil, Sri Lanka, India, and the West Indies. Nutmeg became valuable and was most likely brought to Europe by Arab traders around the sixth century. Nutmegs were carried to ward off all sorts of health problems. The scent will boost clairvoyance and increase your energy level.

Mace

Did you notice that the botanical name of mace *(Myristica fragrans)* is the same as that of nutmeg? This, of course, is because they come from different parts of the same fruit. Mace has its own magical correspondences, though. This herb is associated with the planet Mercury and the element of air. Powdered mace is a great spice to add to apple dishes and old-fashioned cooking. This herb is toxic is large quantities, so use your common sense. A pinch of mace can be worked into herbal sachets to increase mental power and psychic abilities. Both of these herbs, mace and nutmeg, can be worked successfully into any spell to bring clarity and mental sharpness, and, of course, to increase your energy level. Try combining these herbs with a touch of color and candle magic, and see what you can conjure up.

Mace and Nutmeg Candle Spell to Increase Energy

Cast this spell during a waxing moon, to increase your vitality, or a full moon, for more power. Cast on a Tuesday to bring passion and *oomph* to your magic. For this spell you will need:

- 1 orange votive candle, for vitality and to increase energy
- A votive-candle cup holder
- A straight pin or nail to engrave the astrological symbol of Mars ($\male$) into the candle, to help increase your enthusiasm and energy
- A pinch of both powdered mace and nutmeg
- A lighter or some matches
- A flat, safe surface to work on

Carefully carve the symbol of Mars ($\male$) on the side of the votive. Next, sprinkle a smidgen of the two spices in the bottom of the candle cup. Be sure to wipe off your fingers. Set the candle on top of the spices, and light the candle. Repeat this charm three times:

The color orange increases vitality,
A pinch of nutmeg and mace sets the spell free.
Now swirl about, bringing energy to spare,
By these two herbs' elements of fire and air.

You may close this spell with the tag line from chapter 1:

For the good of all, with harm to none.
By herb magic this spell is done.

Allow the candle to burn in a safe place until it is consumed.

Parsley

Parsley *(Petroselinum crispum)* has been a favorite culinary herb for centuries. It is rich in vitamins and minerals, and is a natural breath freshener. The fresh herb adds great color and flavor to many dishes. Its correspondences are the planet Mercury and the element of air. Parsley is associated with the Greek goddess of the underworld, Persephone. This herb has links to honor, health, love, and death. The ancient Greeks and Romans incorporated parsley into many types of social events, from the wedding party's flowers to the herb used at funerals. At ancient feasts, the guests would adorn themselves with garlands and crowns of parsley to stimulate their appetites. Parsley was also thought to add an aura of serenity and calm, creating a relaxing environment.

An interesting bit of folklore states that only a Witch can successfully grow parsley. But I have met plenty of herb gardeners, Witches and not, who have grown a fine patch of parsley in a nice, sunny garden. In addition, this herb may tell you who wears the pants in the family. Herbal folklore states that if parsley flourishes in the herb garden, then the mistress of the house is the one in charge.

A Pot o' Parsley: For Joy and Good Health

If you enjoy having fresh potted herbs on hand in the kitchen for cooking, then try this herb spell. Find a healthy parsley plant, pot it in rich potting soil, and add it to your kitchen. (Make sure you give it plenty of water and a good, sunny location, so it will thrive.) Now use those energies of the parsley plant to create a healthy atmosphere for everyone in your home—at any time. If you'd like to incorporate a bit of astrological timing into this one, cast on a Thursday, to promote healthier energies. Hold your hands over the plant, repeating the following verse three times. This will enchant the plant, encouraging it to boost the environment of your house in a way that promotes prosperity.

> *Bless this parsley plant, so alive and green,*
> *Create peace and banish things oft unseen.*
> *By the magic of herbs this spell is cast,*
> *Bringing joy and health that will surely last.*

If you tend to use a lot of fresh parsley for cooking, I'd probably plant two or three of these to have on hand and enjoy. This spell could be easily adapted to bless parsley plants grown outdoors in your garden too!

Sage

Sage *(Salvia officinalis)* is an aromatic evergreen with textured gray-green leaves. This herb has the planetary association of Jupiter and is linked to the element of air. This ties in neatly for us, as Jupiter is associated with healing, and the element of air can be invoked to bring positive change very quickly into your life. The name sage comes from the Latin word *salvare*, which means "to heal." Sage has a varied and vast herbal tradition. It was used for love divinations and to increase wisdom, grant a long life, ease grief, banish negative entities, and boost fertility. There are folk tales about sage that are similar to those of parsley. For example, there is an old proverb that states: If the sage bush thrives and grows, the master's not master and he knows.

Some older herbal texts claimed that to banish nightmares, the dreamer was supposed to rub fresh sage leaves over his or her body before retiring, to ward off anymore nightmares. I would avoid this old "cure," especially if you have sensitive skin! Carrying fresh sage leaves in your pocket or, if you prefer, tied into a little herbal sachet reinforces your personal protection, promotes good health, and also speeds recovery from illness.

Feeling the need to chase away the blues? Have a walloping case of the blahs? Want to buck up your inner strength and maybe toss in a bit of wisdom while you're at it? Then sage is the herb for you. For the following charm you can either work with fresh sage leaves from the garden or produce section, or simply incorporate the powdered dry herb from the spice rack—it's up to you.

Burning Away the Blues: An Herbal Candle Spell

For best results, work this spell during a waning moon. As the moon decreases, so will your depression. You will need:

- 1 blue, 6-inch taper-style candle, or a blue mini taper (often sold in metaphysical stores as spell candles)
- A coordinating candle holder
- A handful of fresh or dried sage leaves
- A saucer or small plate
- A lighter or some matches
- A safe, flat surface to work on

After the spell is completed, you will also need:

- A blue ink pen
- A plain envelope

Set the taper in the holder, and place that in the center of the plate. Then sprinkle a small amount of the powdered herb (on the saucer) in a circle around the base of the candle holder. Or else, arrange the fresh leaves in a loose circle around the candle holder. Wipe off your hands to remove any dried herbs, and then light the blue candle.

Take a moment to visualize yourself surrounded by a bright, sparkling shield of energy. This light pulses from your body like an aura, and attracts only positive and healthy things to you. Hold this visualization for a few moments until you begin to feel a little warmer. Now open your eyes and repeat this spell:

Sage, herb of wisdom, help remove the blues,
Grant me strength, good health, and clear vision true.
A bright blue candle for peace and to encourage strength,
This spell burns true as the candle reduces its length.
Once gone, all dis-ease is removed far from me,
And as I do will it, then so must it be!

Allow the candle to burn out in a safe place, making sure to keep an eye on it. When the candle has burned away, gather up the sage and put it into a plain envelope. Seal it, and write on the outside of the envelope your name, the healing and astrological symbol of Jupiter (♃), and your magical intention. Then tuck the envelope in your purse, pocket, notebook, or briefcase, and allow the energy of the herbs to stay with you for a few days.

After a few days have passed, take the envelope outside, tear it open, and scatter the herbs to the wind. Call on the element of air to help speed wisdom and healing on their way. When you are finished, dispose of the envelope neatly in a garbage can.

Charming Plants You May Not Know Are Herbs

Our attitude toward life determines life's attitude toward us.

—EARL NIGHTINGALE

Dianthus

Also known as clove pinks, dianthus *(Dianthus carophyllus)* are easy-to-grow perennials that come in lovely pastel shades and hot pink and make charming front-of-the-border flowers in a sunny garden. This plant has the planetary correspondence of the Sun and the elemental association of fire, making it both a healing plant and an energy restorer.

Dianthus is the parent plant of what we know today as carnations. So in a pinch, you can always pick up a few inexpensive stems of mini carnations at the florist, and these will work just as well in your herb magic. Add these fragrant petals to sachets and charm bags as an energy booster. The ancient Greeks and Romans wore these fragrant little flowers as garlands and floral crowns. On an interesting herbal note, *carnation* and *coronation* come from the same root word.

Here is an herbal spell designed to boost your energy and allow you to heal. This is a great spell for when you are sending healing energy to another, or if you are trying to shake a nasty cold or flu bug.

In the Pink: A Healing Spell

For this herbal spell, you will need a few stems of flowers from the dianthus plant. Or you can simply pick up a few inexpensive stems of hot-pink, spicy-scented mini carnations at the local florist. If you choose to use regular, full-sized carnations, that's okay too. For best results, work this spell on a Sunday, the day of the Sun, or try a Thursday, Jupiter's day, to promote robustness and recovery.

Arrange the flowers in a small, water-filled vase. That way, if you are working this spell for another, you can easily give the simple flower arrangement as a gift. If you don't want to bother with arranging the flowers, have a florist arrange a few carnations in a vase for you. (Typically, single carnations are inexpensive, and many florists will be happy to arrange a few stems in a bud vase for a small fee, while you wait.)

Once you have the flowers arranged to your liking, hold your hands out and over the flowers. Repeat the following charm three times, and visualize that you are charging the blossoms to make them last longer and to heighten their natural healing properties. Basically, this is a sort of energy exchange between you and the flowers. You are blessing the flowers with a longer bloom time, and in return they are sending you (or the intended recipient) some healing energy.

Through these pink, spicy blooms, I send out energy,
With a touch of herbal aromatherapy.
Bless me (them) with health,
May my words quickly create a link.
Now may this scented herbal charm,
put me (them) "in the pink."

Next, either set the vase in a spot where you can enjoy it
and see it often, or give the flowers as a gift with your best
wishes for a speedy recovery.

Purple Coneflower

In most herb magic books, the coneflower *(Echinacea pur-
purea* and *Echinacea augustifolia)* is never given a planetary
or elemental correspondence. Since this is one of my favorite flowers, I quickly made up my mind to fix that right
here and now. I feel that the coneflower corresponds beautifully to the Sun and the element of fire. Why did I choose
these correlations? I have a few reasons. The shape of the
flower reminds me of a sun with rays shooting out from all
around it. Coneflowers flourish in sunny spots, and it is
very drought-tolerant. Therefore, this astrological association made sense to me as a gardener. I chose the element of
fire because it linked nicely to the Sun. Echinacea is a healing herb, and healers will call on the element of fire to remove impurities and for transformation.

Purple coneflowers are a wildflower native to much of the
central United States. These hardy perennial flowers are easy
to find at garden centers and nurseries. These no-nonsense

flowers perform wonderfully in many different types of sun-exposure gardens. Coneflowers will bloom their best in full sun, but they tolerate part shade as well. They are well worth having in any magical garden, as they have a long blooming time, make excellent cut flowers, and attract bees and butterflies to the garden. Plus, when the flowers fade in the fall, the goldfinches love to snack on the thistles in the cone.

The purple coneflower is one of those flowers that many gardeners grow and then later discover has magical properties. Myself included. I was given several clumps of this perennial when I first began gardening. It was only a few years later that I discovered there was much more to one of my favorite flowers than I had first realized.

Coneflowers may be incorporated into herbal spells and charms for strength and healing. Plus, the flowers can be used magically to strengthen spells of any kind. For this next herbal sachet, you may work with either fresh coneflowers or dried cones and petals.

Herbal Sachet to Promote Health

For this sachet, choose whatever color you associate with healing magic for the bag, ribbon, and fabric. Some magical folks like green, red, or blue. This is your choice, and it makes the magic uniquely your own. You may work this spell on a Thursday, Jupiter's day, or a Sunday, to pull in some solar energies. If you want to add lunar energies to this magic, you can cast during a waxing moon, to promote an increase of health and to pull in more healing energies, or a waning moon, to remove the illness. This basic rule of thumb can be applied to all the spells in this chapter.

Add into the bag several healing herbs. (Try the ones featured in this chapter, or check the correspondence lists in the appendix.) Then tuck in a coneflower to boost the magical properties of all the other herbs and to strengthen the "punch" of the charm.

Now hold the herb-filled bag in the palms of your hands, and enchant it for healing with this verse:

I charge these herbs for comfort, health, and power,
All with the help of the purple coneflower.

Tie the bag closed and knot it three times, while saying this traditional closing line:

By power of three times three,
As I will it, so must it be.

Keep the herbal charm bag on your person for one week. Then open the bag, and neatly return the contents to nature.

Herbal Trees to Promote Well-Being

There is something witchlike in the appearance of witch hazel . . .
—HENRY DAVID THOREAU

Witch Hazel

Witch hazel *(Hamamelis virginiana)* is associated with the Sun and the element of fire. This small tree blooms in early spring and is lovely in many landscapes. It is one of the first trees to bloom each year, which is how it earned the name "winterbloom." In the Midwest, where I live, the witch hazels start to bloom in late February. It's not unusual to see those bright-yellow ribbonlike blossoms covered with a dusting of snow.

According to herbal tradition, witch hazel is the preferred material to use when crafting diving rods. A diving rod made out of the forked branches of this herbal tree could point you to water or gold. The forty-niners in particular used this method. Carrying a few fresh leaves or the blossoms of the witch hazel helps heal a broken heart.

For this next herbal spell, you are going to have to go on a hunt for a witch hazel tree. Try the local park, or ask around the neighborhood and see if anyone has one growing in their yard. This spell is meant to be worked outdoors, and it will require you to go outside and stand or sit under a healthy witch hazel tree.

Witch Hazel Tree Spell to Mend a Broken Heart

Once you have located a witch hazel tree, *gently* gather a fallen leaf or a blossom or two. Don't strip the tree. Not only is that rude, but you should remember that this is a living thing, so treat it with respect. A single leaf will work just fine. It's the quality, not the quantity, that counts. Now, hold the leaf or blossom in the palms of your hands. Feel its warm and soothing energy flow through your hands and out into the rest of your body. Finally, hold the foliage to your heart, and repeat this charm three times:

Witch hazel, witch hazel, mend my broken heart,
Now, chase sadness away, with this Witch's art.
Bring comfort, healing, and joy, lift up my spirits please,
Help me to move on, by the power of three times three.

When you are finished, leave an offering to the witch hazel tree, such as a small crystal, a bit of birdseed for the birds, or a strand of your hair. Or you could pick up any trash in the vicinity and make the tree's home a cleaner and happier environment.

Ash

The deciduous ash tree *(Fraxinus excelsior* or *Fraxinus americana)* is classically associated with the Sun and the element of fire. The ash is the great world tree, known as Yggdrasill. The Norse gods Odin and Thor are associated with the ash, as was the Greek goddess Nemesis. Nemesis carried an ash rod that symbolized divine justice. This herbal tree is associated with rebirth and new life. In some magical traditions, the ash tree was associated with the element of water, which explains its links to another of the Greek gods—Poseidon, god of the sea. In many various types of magical traditions, the ash is utilized as an energy restorer and a health-giving source.

The ash is a healing tree, so two ash twigs may be fashioned into a solar amulet, and the solar energies used to help fight off the wintertime blues, also known as seasonal affective disorder. There are many folks who feel down in the dumps during the long winter months. The darkest days of the year and a lack of opportunity to be outside in colder climates can really contribute to a walloping case of the blahs.

For those of us who are gardeners and who love the natural world, there is a lot of sulking going on during the bitter cold days of January and February. The quickest way to perk yourself up is to soak up a little winter sunshine. Technically, this is know as "bright light therapy."

If it's too cold to walk outside for an hour, then spend some time indoors near a sunny window, and absorb some solar energy. Try to do this as often as you can, like the next time you are on your lunch break. Find a sunny spot indoors, and go soak up some sunshine. If you can get outside without freezing your rear off, then bundle up and walk around the neighborhood for a bit, or run a few errands. Take advantage of those sunlit winter days and the healing energies of the sunlight as often as you can.

Herbal Solar Amulet

The directions for creating and enchanting a solar amulet made out of ash are beautifully simple. Create this amulet on a nice, sunny day. Take two small ash twigs about six inches in length, and tie them together into an equal-armed cross (also known as a solar cross). Fasten a gold ribbon at the center of the twigs, and knot the ribbon three times, saying:

> *By the powers of the ash tree, herb magic, and the sun,*
> *Do as I will, bringing harm to none.*

Then hold the amulet up to the sunshine, and bless it with the following charm to ward off the winter blues and to encourage healing:

> *I take two ash twigs, and tie a ribbon round,*
> *A simple solar amulet I have bound.*
> *Bring sunshine to my life and guard me, I pray,*
> *Keeping those wintertime blues far, far away.*

You can hang this amulet in a prominent location in your home, or tuck it into your locker or desk at work. This amulet would also be easy to adapt to a pocket charm, if you keep the twigs about two inches in length. Now, you have yourself a little, portable solar amulet.

Garden Witchery: From Garden to Cauldron

> *Plant me a garden to heal the heart,*
> *Balm for joy, and the sweet violet*
> *Cowslip, pansies and chamomile*
> *To ease the pain I want to forget.*

—ELIZABETHAN HERB SONG

Lady's Mantle

The planetary correspondence for the lady's mantle *(Alchemilla mollis)* is Venus, and the elemental correspondence is water. This gorgeous, part-shade-loving perennial makes a wonderful front-of-the-border specimen. At one time, lady's mantle was used as a sort of natural pharmacy. It was often referred to as "a woman's best friend," and was utilized for menstrual problems. It was also valued for its wound-healing abilities, as it was believed to cause blood to clot more quickly.

This plant was thought to possess particular magical powers, as its pleated blue-green leaves collect dew and raindrops, and hold the drops so they look like quicksilver on the fuzzy surface. One of my favorite things to do with this garden plant is to collect and utilize the dewdrops that tremble in the center of the leaves. I just dip my fingers into the dewdrops and then touch the water to my forehead or onto a charm bag, for a little extra herbal enchantment.

The botanical name of this herb, *Alchemilla*, means "the little magical one," and is the root for the word *alchemy*. The name *lady's mantle* came from the shape of the leaves, which were thought to resemble a lady's flowing cloak.

Tucking a soft, fuzzy leaf or two into a charm bag or herbal sachet would be a wonderful way to add some healing properties to the mix. You may work with either the leaves or the lime-green flowers that appear in the early summer.

Herbal Sachet for Healing

You may work this herbal spell on any day or during any moon phase. As mentioned before, if you are working for healing and you cast during a waxing moon, visualize that you are pulling positive energy toward you. If you cast during the waning moon, push the negativity and illness away. For this spell, you will need six healing herbs, some lady's mantle foliage or flowers, and a green cloth sachet bag.

(Make your own sachet bag, or try using one of those organza favor bags.)

Gather together six herbs of your choosing that bring comfort and promote good health. Then add the lady's mantle foliage or flowers. Tie up the sachet bag, and knot the ribbon closed three times. Hold the sachet in your hands, and focus on the four elements of earth, air, fire, and water. Picture these energies spinning around you in a bright, glowing ring. Then repeat this charm:

> *Little magical one, add your power to this mix,*
> *Any sickness or despair you will certainly nix.*
> *I bless this sachet with the magic of land and sea,*
> *Empowered by the air and fire, so mote it be.*

Keep the herbal sachet on your person for one week. Then open the bag, say a quiet thank you to the elements, and neatly return the contents to nature. You may handwash the organza bag, allow it to air-dry, and then reuse it another time.

Feverfew

Feverfew *(Tanacetum parthenium)* has the magical correspondences of the planet Venus and the element of water. This herb was known to the ancient Greeks, and supposedly acquired its name from the tale that a worker fell off the top of the Parthenon and survived. This herb was used in the treatment that saved the person's life. The common name comes from the Latin words *febris,* which means "fever," and *fugure,* which means "to chase away."

The fifteenth-century herbalists used the fresh leaves of the feverfew to cure "swimming of the head"—in other words, migraines. The feverfew leaves are generally considered safe for consumption. However, I'd still be wary of possible side effects, such as an allergic reaction. I suggest growing this herb as an ornamental. Be safe and don't doctor yourself, family, or friends with it.

Feverfew is a wonderful garden perennial. It makes huge masses of tiny, white, daisy-looking flowers that work well in floral arrangements. I use these dainty blossoms as filler in herbal bouquets, instead of baby's breath. A mature feverfew plant makes hundreds of blossoms, and each of those flowers will drop lots of seeds—and will then reseed all over the place in your garden. To avoid this scenario, deadhead (trim) the flower heads off the plants as soon as they fade. These flowers are beautiful in bloom and are well worth the effort required to thin them out from all the babies they make.

Feverfew flowers mingle well in the garden with roses and lavender. One of my herb books states that feverfew "reseeds itself generously." That's an understatement. This flowering herb reseeds all over the place, so don't be bashful about pulling up new plants, thinning them out, and moving them around. Feverfew blooms in late summer and again in early fall if you snip off the spent flower heads. This gardening chore is called deadheading.

Health Protection Charm: A Feverfew Spell

Carrying the blossoms of the feverfew wards of colds and flu. Try tucking a bit of this flowering herb into your hair, or pin it in your buttonhole, like a tiny corsage. Enchant the fresh flowers with this quick, little health-protection charm:

> *Tiny flowers, lovely and white,*
> *Ward off colds and flu both day and night.*

Chamomile

Chamaemelum nobile is sometimes referred to as "true" or Roman chamomile. This perennial type of chamomile creeps or grows low to the ground. On the other hand, German chamomile *(Matricaria recutita)* is an annual plant that grows taller and is upright. Chamomile has the magical correspondences of the Sun and the element of water. When grown in a sunny garden, this plant has the ability to protect the home and its occupants.

Using prepackaged chamomile tea is a great way to work herb magic quickly and inexpensively. You can purchase prepackaged chamomile teas at most grocery stores. This comforting tea is popular for soothing frazzled nerves and helping induce sleep and dreaming. As with all pre-packaged herbal teas, consult your physician before using chamomile if you are pregnant or taking a prescription.

I do grow chamomile in my garden, and it always surprises me by reseeding itself in between the bricks in the front garden's path. A brave little chamomile flower pops up here and there throughout the summer. I enjoy these delicate, apple-scented flowers for as long as they last (before one of my kids steps on them).

A little sea salt and a few fresh chamomile flowers may be added to your bath water to remove negativity, soothe the senses, and help you unwind after a long day. Please note that while chamomile is mild, it may irritate sensitive skin. Try a little test patch on the inside of your arm first. Make up a weak tea, and swab it on the inside of your elbow. Wait a few hours to see if there is any reaction—better to find out ahead of time than after you've soaked your whole body in the tub.

A Soothing Herbal Bath

Fill the tub with comfortably warm water, toss in a few fresh chamomile flowers, and stir in a teaspoon of sea salt. (The salt will open your pores and make you perspire—so don't go overboard with it. It can cause you to become lightheaded.) Note: If you are pregnant or nursing, you will want to skip the herbs and the salt. Add a half cup of milk to the water instead, to soothe and soften the skin. Put the chamomile in a small vase nearby, and enjoy the sweet apple scent of these tiny flowers.

Next, lower yourself into the water, and repeat this charm:

Chamomile flowers added to a nice hot bath,
Bring relaxation and health that will surely last.
Add a pinch of salt to remove negativity,
May tranquility and beauty now swirl around me.

When the water cools or you finish your bath, dry off and slip into something comfy. To complete your indulgence, go do something you find relaxing. Take the afternoon or evening off. Sip a glass of wine or juice, read a good book, or listen to some soothing music. Claim this time as your own and just unwind, because you *do* deserve it.

Courage and perseverance have a magical talisman, before which difficulties disappear and obstacles vanish into air.

—JOHN QUINCY ADAMS

CHAPTER FIVE

HERB MAGIC FOR PROTECTION

Herbs are filled with positive magical energy, and they naturally ward off bad vibes, negativity, and manipulative magics. While you work with herbs for protection, remember that these plants will help negativity to literally "bounce" off you. So, the next logical questions are, just where is all this negativity bouncing to? And what do you do about it?

Well, you have some options. Some of these options you may like, but others you may find not to your taste. So here they are. You can return negative energy to its sender. (Some folks don't have a problem with this, but others will be up in arms at my mentioning it.) Or, you can ask for the universe to absorb it harmlessly. I know one clever Witch who takes bad luck or negative energy and then transforms it into something positive. Finally, you could drive the negativity away and then safely dissolve it. It is completely up to you.

Obviously, the conscientious magic user is not going to want to purposely harm another, even with a boomerang-type of situation, so I think the "drive it away, then make it dissolve" scenario is the best way to go. And in case you're wondering, that's what I typically do.

While working protective magic, the three best lunar phases to work in are the full moon, for more power; the waning moon, to make the problem shrink and dissolve; and the dark of the moon, for banishing really intense situations. The best day of the week for protection magic is Saturday. Saturday is associated with Saturn, a god of karma and time. Plus, this is the final day of the week, and you can neatly tap into that day's energies to bring the negative situation to an end. The astrological symbol for Saturn is ♄, and it could be added into most of these herbal charms and spells for protection. Or, if you want to banish fear and have a sort of spiritual-warrior mindset, you could incorporate the symbol for Mars (♂), and pull in some passion and bravery.

The most important thing to remember while working protection magic is to not let your fears get the best of you. Dig down deep, grab hold of your courage with both hands, and work your herb magic to create positive change.

Protection Spells from the Spice Rack

Courage is resistance to fear, mastery of fear—not absence of fear.
—MARK TWAIN

Anise

The magical correspondences for anise *(Pimpinella anisum)* are the planet Mars and the element of fire. This annual herb is easy to grow from seed in a sunny location. When this plant reaches maturity, it stands about twenty inches in height and resembles a sort of spindly Queen Anne's lace. Its leaves are rounded at the base and narrow at the stem. The flowers are small, white, starlike clusters, described in most herb books as "umbels." The fruit follows the flowering, and it is the dried fruit or the seeds that are used in cooking. Anise is a popular spice is East Indian cooking. It is often used to flavor sweets, liquors, and fruit dishes.

This licorice-scented herb is used for protection. Placing fresh anise leaves in a room will remove negativity and drive away evil. When the leaves are positioned in a bedroom, they banish nightmares. If you like the scent, try tucking the leaves or seeds into a dream pillow.

Anise seeds may be cast on the ground to create a magic circle of protection. Also, the foliage or seeds may be carried or tucked into herbal sachets or charm bags for security and to prevent the evil eye.

Sachet Bag for Protection and Pleasant Dreams

To link all of the magical correspondences together, create this sachet bag and perform this spell on a Tuesday. This Mars day brings bravery and the courage to face your fears. Choose a scarlet-red color for the fabric of the sachet or the ribbons to fasten it closed. Draw the symbol for Mars (♂) on the outside of the sachet bag with a permanent marker. Then, carefully add the anise seeds and/or fresh leaves to the bag. Once the anise is contained inside the sachet, enchant the bag for protection using this simple charm:

> *Tiny anise seeds have a distinct, powerful scent,*
> *Tied up in a bag of red, evil they will prevent.*
> *I am protected and safe, both night and day,*
> *All with the help of a bewitching sachet.*

You can carry this sachet bag with you in your pocket or purse, or set it on your nightstand, or tuck it under your pillow to ensure pleasant dreams.

Please note: The scent will be strong, so make sure you enjoy the smell of anise before you try to sleep with it under your pillow.

Sweet Bay

Sweet bay *(Laurus nobilis)* has the planetary correspondence of the Sun. Its elemental association is fire. This solar herb of purification was sacred to the sun god Apollo. The fragrant branches were once incorporated into a chaplet or wreath that was worn around the head. Apollo was depicted as wearing a wreath of bay, and in ancient times, his devotees did the same. Greek and Roman scholars, poets, and victorious soldiers wore this fragrant herb as well.

The bay leaf was employed as a strewing herb, and was often burned in homes, as the smoke was believed to fight off infection and help keep insects away. A bay leaf will protect its bearer from negativity and evil.

Bay can be grown in a pot as a small clipped plant, like a topiary, or in warmer climates it can be grown as a tree. According to herbal tradition, no negative magic, thunder, or lightning could ever harm a person in a place where a bay tree was planted. Today, culinary bay leaves are often added to beef, stews, soups, and chili to enhance the flavor of these dishes. They can also be added to a magical herbalist's spells for protection.

Bay Leaf Spell to Keep Ghosts and Negativity at Bay

Yes, I will admit it, that was a shameless play on words. It's okay to chuckle while you learn about herb magic. Sometimes having a sense of humor and a light heart is the best protection magic anyone could possibly conjure.

Now, to employ a touch of bay leaf magic in your life, burn the fragrant leaves to banish negativity, ghosts, and poltergeists. The best day of the week for this type of magic would be Sunday, to tap into the solar aspects of the herb, or Tuesday, for passion and courage, and to link to a warrior type of energy. Or you could work on Saturday—the best day of the week for banishings—to really do some ghost busting. Since bay is associated with fire, a touch of fire magic works well here. Place the dried bay leaf in a fireproof dish, a small metal cauldron, or even a terra-cotta plant saucer.

To begin, hold the leaf in your hand, and name it for the problem by saying, "This bay leaf represents the negativity" (or represents the ghosts, etc.). Then place it in the fireproof dish and set it aflame with a lighter or match. Repeat this charm as the leaf burns away:

> *By the power of fire this leaf burns away,*
> *Spirits are banished, trouble is removed today.*

Bay Leaf Spell to Promote Courage

For this enchantment, the timing would be the same as the first bay leaf spell. To promote courage and protection, you may write a wish on a bay leaf and then burn it for good luck. (I suggest using a felt-tipped pen, so you won't tear the leaf.) Try this bay leaf charm to encourage those fortunate and positive qualities in your life:

> *I write my wishes on a bay leaf so green,*
> *Send courage and protection quickly to me.*

As the leaf burns away, this spell is begun,
By the powers of fire and the bright sun.

When the ashes are cool, take them outside, close your eyes, and then blow the ashes gently away to the winds.

Dill

Dill *(Anethum graveolens)* is an annual herb aligned with the planet Mercury and the element of fire. Dill is a fun herb to grow in the home garden or in pots and containers in a sunny location. It grows over two feet in height and is a wonderful accent plant in the middle of a container full of magical herbs. This herb is a lovely shade of green and has feathery, threadlike foliage. It bears yellow flowers in late summer to early fall. In medieval times, dill seeds were chewed to relieve hunger pains and as a breath freshener. Dill was used to flavor vinegars and as a pickling spice, and it seasoned many a culinary dish, such as fish, salads, and sauces.

Dill was used by ancient peoples in Egypt, Greece, and Italy. The Egyptians first used this as a medicinal herb 5,000 years ago, and the Romans and Greeks grew this herb in their own kitchen gardens. Dill grew wild in Britain in Saxon times, and on an interesting note, the name dill comes from the Anglo-Saxon word *dylle,* which means "to lull or soothe."

According to some of the oldest herbals, dill was used in magic for love potions, and was hung in bunches to promote protection and prosperity in the home. For example, dill was hung above a baby's bed for protection. This herb was a magical "big gun," as folks believed that it could repel even the most evil of spells and curses. Today, the fragrant flower heads may be tucked into charm bags and herbal sachets to promote clear thinking, security, and safety.

A Triple Goddess Herbal Warding Spell

For the biggest magical punch, work this spell on the full moon. If you can't wait that long, try a Tuesday, to invoke courage and defense, or a Saturday, for protection and banishing. Once you have the bag filled, you will be placing or hanging the sachet by the main entrance to your home to prevent bad luck or negativity from entering. This type of magic is referred to as *warding.* Warding means that you are setting in place a sort of magical alarm system that will alert you to anyone or anything that tries to enter uninvited into your home.

You will need the following supplies:

- A few tablespoons of dill, for protection and to denote a magical safe house
- A few leaves of St. John's wort, for protection against enchantment
- A three-leaf clover, for good luck and because it is a triple-goddess symbol
- A tablespoon of dried vervain, to make the spell "go" (dried vervain can be found at most metaphysical shops)

- A 6-inch square of red fabric
- 12 inches each of red, white, and black satin ribbons

Combine the four herbal ingredients, and place in the center of the fabric. Gather up the sides, and tie the bundle closed with the red, white, and black ribbons for protection, and to invoke the Triple Goddess. If you really want to personalize this spell, you could draw with a black marker or even embroider on the red fabric the triple-moon symbol (☽○☾). This will help link the herb magic back to the Triple Goddess, and will empower the herbs even more. Knot the ribbons closed three times, saying:

> *One knot each for the Maiden, Mother, and Crone,*
> *Bless this protective charm that I've made on my own.*

Then hang the herb-filled bag inside your home, next to the main entrance. Once it's in place, set up the wards with this verse:

> *St. John's wort, vervain, clover, and dill,*
> *Ward well my home, protect from ill will.*
> *Make this house a secure magical place,*
> *Defend and protect us through time and space.*

Visualize a bright, protective light surrounding your doorway. Tap the bag of herbs three times to activate the spell. You may refresh this warding spell every six months or so.

Garlic

Garlic *(Allium sativum)* is associated with the planet Mars and the element of fire. This herb is sacred to the triple goddess Hecate, and it was often left at the crossroads as an offering to her. Garlic was also associated with the god Mars, as Roman soldiers ate the herb to increase their courage and strength. The Anglo-Saxon roots of the word garlic are *gar*, "spear," which is probably a description of the long, green onionlike foliage that shoots up from the bulb; and *leac*, a term that denotes a pot herb.

One of the oldest plants known to humanity, garlic has healing qualities. It contains iron and vitamins, and is a mild natural antiseptic. Not surprisingly, one of the old folk names for garlic is "heal all." According to herbal folklore, people wore a clove of garlic as an amulet to ward off the plague. They also used it to defend against vampires, to keep sailors safe at sea, and to protect its bearer from Witchcraft. In some cultures, garlic was used as an aphrodisiac, and it was thought to boost the male libido.

In the kitchen, garlic has been used for centuries. I finally took the plunge and starting cooking with fresh garlic a few years ago. It's a great seasoning to add, as garlic mellows as it cooks and becomes sweeter. If you've never cooked with fresh garlic before, you should give it a try.

Braided garlic may be hung in the kitchen to provide protection for the family and to promote well-being and contentment. Garlic is one of the best protective herbs, and hung over doorways in your home, it will fight negativity, absorb evil, and ward off spiteful people, psychic vampires, and roaming ghosts. Try adding one of those decorative braids of garlic to your kitchen to ward and protect the heart of your home.

Kitchen Witch Braided Garlic Charm

You can work this quick Kitchen Witch spell at any time and during any moon phase. Hang the braided garlic in the kitchen, and enchant it for protection and to encourage a happy, healthy home with the following charm:

> *I enchant this braid of garlic so fine,*
> *Keep negativity out at all times.*
> *Psychic vampires, roaming ghouls, and ghosts beware,*
> *You will never find refuge in this Witch's lair!*

Sure, this charm is a little tongue-in-cheek, but remember that laughter can be the best positive type of magic that you could ever hope to tap into. If you really want to take the wind out of the sails of someone who is trying to frighten you or make you miserable, just laugh. Then, forget about the person.

Warding Plants You May Not Know Are Herbs

> *Open afresh your round of starry folds,*
> *Ye ardent marigolds!*
> *Dry up the moisture from your golden lids,*
> *For great Apollo bids . . .*

—KEATS

Calendula (Pot Marigold)

Calendula *(Calendula officinalis)*, also called pot marigold, is an annual flowering herb that corresponds to the Sun

and the element of fire. To the Hindus, this flower represented eternal life and health. Herbal legend says the name
of the plant came from a young Greek maiden called
Caltha. She saw the sun god, Apollo, and fell hopelessly in
love. She became obsessed with him, and every day she
waited for the sun to appear, hoping to catch another
glimpse of the god. Alas, she never saw him, and she eventually wasted away. To honor her devotion, the first marigold
appeared on the spot where she died.

In ancient times, people wore garlands of the pot marigold
at wedding feasts, and it was a popular flower to bring indoors, as it was considered a lucky blossom to have. In modern times, carrying a calendula in your pocket will help you
find justice and favor in court. The sunshine-colored blossoms were also believed to strengthen the eyesight, drive
away all negative thoughts, and promote joy and a positive
attitude. In fact, the old herbalists believed that just sitting
and studying the bright orange flowers growing in the garden was a sure-fire way to banish the blues.

They best time to gather pot marigolds for magical
working is at noon on a sunny day. Scatter the loose petals
in the bedroom to keep nightmares away. This little flower
is a powerful herb to be be used in any protection charm or
spell.

Petal Power

Here is an herbal charm to protect your abode and ward
the thresholds of your home. You can cast this spell on any

sunny day, but try it on a Sunday for extra success and power. Gather together a handful of fresh calendula petals at noon, to tap into the amazing strength and positive power of the sun. Take a moment to hold these lovely orange petals in your hands, and feel the punch of energy that comes from their scent and color. Now bless these petals for protection, and scatter them across the thresholds of your home, or across your front and back porches, while you repeat this charm:

> *As I cast these flower petals on the ground,*
> *No negativity shall ever be found.*
> *Orange for vitality and energy to spare,*
> *My home is protected, with an herbalist's flair.*

Close the protection charm with this line:

> *By the shining power of the sun,*
> *So mote it be and let it harm none.*

Holly

The familiar holly bush (*Ilex* ssp.) is an extremely lucky and protective herb. It is associated with the planet Mars and the element of fire. The holly was a sacred plant to the Druids, and was a popular natural decoration for midwinter festivities in many magical cultures.

The Romans used holly wreaths for their Saturnalia festivals. In Europe, the evergreen holly was considered a masculine plant, and was incorporated into winter solstice celebrations along with its feminine counterpart, ivy. Since holly was such a magical plant, there were certain rules that needed to be followed while "decking the halls." Holly was not to be brought in the house before the winter solstice and had to be removed on Twelfth Night, which is January 6. These twelve days of partying were the forerunners of the twelve days of Christmas. As long as holly was displayed inside the home, it was believed that the faeries of winter would use this as a temporary home. The faeries were believed to enjoy the break from the cold and then would bless the family with good luck and good fortune in the coming year.

When this shrub is planted around the home, it brings protection to the entire household. Holly also has the reputation of protecting folks from lightning strikes, manipulative magic, ghosts, and unethical sorcerers.

Holly Spell for Protection

For this spell, you will need three red, pillar-type candles, a sprig of berried holly, a small slip of paper, and an ink pen. Arrange the candles on a large plate, and nestle in the sprig of holly at the center base. Set the plate on a safe, flat surface, and light the candles. Since the holly is associated with Mars, the best day of the week to work this spell is a Tuesday, to help increase bravery and to tap into the warrior's spirit. As always when it comes to protection magic, use a waxing moon to pull protection toward you, and a waning moon to banish your fears and dread.

Once you have the candles lit, take a moment to focus on the problem, and write it down on the slip of paper. Carefully draw the astrological symbol for Mars ($\mathcal{O}^{7}$) at the top of the paper. Fold the paper and then *carefully* drip a bit of the melting wax on the paper. (Be cautious—don't burn yourself.) Next, tuck the sealed slip of paper neatly under one of the candles. Then repeat this spell:

> *A trio of scarlet candles burning so bright,*
> *Brings radiance and comfort on the darkest nights.*
> *The sacred holly protects, guards, and defends,*
> *All worries and troubles now come to an end.*
> *By all the power of three times three,*
> *As I will it, then so shall it be.*

Let the candles burn for a few hours. You can let them burn until they are gone, or just relight them every night for a few hours until they burn themselves out. It's up to you. Once the candles burn out, burn the slip of paper to ash in a small metal pot or cauldron. (Do this outside.) After the slip of paper is consumed, wait a few moments and then scatter the cool ashes to the wind.

Lamb's Ears (Betony)

Lamb's ears are a modern cousin to the ancient plant known as betony *(Stachys officinalis)*. Betony is associated with the planet Jupiter and the element of fire. According to older herbal texts, this herb could drive away night terrors and disturbing visions and dreams. The Anglo-Saxons wore the silvery leaves as a charm against evil spirits.

Today, lamb's ears are an easy-to-find and affordable alternative to betony. This easy-to-grow perennial will add protection to your home. Dried, crumbled leaves scattered across the threshold may be used to reinforce a home's security. I have been working with this herb for years, and I have found that lamb's ears have the same magical qualities as the old betony. I will warn you, however, that this silvery and soft blooming herb spreads like crazy in the garden. One small plant will quadruple in size by the end of the growing season. The flower spikes can grow up to three feet in height and have small purple flowers on the stalks. Lamb's ears will perform well in either full sun or part shade. This does makes a wonderful front-of-the-garden plant, and children love to pet the soft, fuzzy "ears."

Betony Charm for Security

Crumble the fuzzy leaves of perennial lamb's ears (betony) around the outside of your home for security. These form a barrier that will prevent most bad vibes, negative energies, and manipulations from making their way to your property. You can perform this spell at any time and during any moon phase.

Lamb's ears also make a nice accent color in a flower arrangement, and if you wish, you can tuck in a few silver leaves or the bloom spikes in arrangements. Enchant these herbs to create a sacred space and to protect your home. Try this simple sacred space/protection charm when you work with this herb:

Soft, silver, and fuzzy is betony, the plant called lamb's ears,
They create a border of magic, no evil can draw near.
Lend your lovely power to mine,

Combine through time and space,
This home is protected, as I stand now in sacred space.

Herbal Trees for Security and Protection

Elder is the Lady's tree, burn it not, or cursed you'll be.

—ANONYMOUS, *THE POEM OF THE NINE WOODS*

Elder

Elder *(Sambucus canadensis)* has the planetary correspondence of Venus and is aligned with water. The elder is a deciduous shrubby tree with musk-scented wood and foliage.
This enchanting tree bears beautiful off-white flowers in
the summer, followed by burgundy-colored berries in the
autumn. The berries are incorporated into pies, jams, jellies, and wines. The elder tree is sacred to Venus, Holda,
and many other goddesses. As the opening quote warns,
this tree should be treated with respect. The old herbalists
used elder for all sorts of medical cures, and gathered its
wood and fruit carefully and with ceremony. You are to ask
the Elder Mother, who resides within the elder, three times
for her permission before harvesting from this magical tree.

Wearing the blossoms of the elder imparts protection.
In Scotland, elder branches hung over doorways protect the
entire household. If grown in the yard, the elder tree will
help enforce a kind of magical security throughout your
property. It was said that Witches and spirits dwelled
within the elder. One of the best things about the elder tree
is that its foliage, blossoms, and berries may be worked into
spells that will help break any magics that may have been

cast against you. According to herbal tradition, if you gather these on the night of a full moon, your protection magic will be doubly powerful.

Breaking Spells with the Elder

Here is an elder tree spell that will break an enchantment cast by another. It's up to you how you'd like to set this up. Put your own creative spin on it. You can scatter the foliage or berries around a candle, or tuck them into protection charm bags. Then repeat the following verse three times:

I call upon the spirit of the Elder Mother,
Help me to break this spell, which was cast by another.
Their magic quickly fades, malevolence now ends,
As safety, protection, and harmony begin.

Add the tag line from chapter 1 to close the spell:

For the good of all, with harm to none.
By herb magic this spell is done.

Birch

The white birch tree *(Betula alba)* corresponds to the planet Venus and the element of water. This tree is called the Lady tree and is the female counterpart to the masculine oak. This tree also has been associated with the Norse god Thor. Today, birch leaves may be worked into any charm bag or enchantment for security and safety.

The white birch has many links to magic. Birch is a traditional wood for a ceremonial besom (broom), as it is protective and repels negativity. The tall trunk of the birch tree is often used to create a May pole, and is also a popular wood, due to its white papery bark, for creating a Yule log. Wearing a sprig of birch leaves on Beltane or Midsummer's Night will grant you visions of the faeries.

Branches of the birch tree were often hung over doorways to the home to protect the occupants and to prevent misfortune from entering. Birch branches were thought to ward the home, repel ghosts, and protect from the evil eye and from lightning strikes. Sometimes bundles of birch branches were arranged at the four corners of a person's property, bound together with strips of red cloth, for the same reasons.

Tie a Red Ribbon 'Round the Old Birch Tree

You may tie a red ribbon on a birch tree branch and make a request for protection to the god Thor. Thor is a good choice for working spells to boost your own magical shields and for enchantments that require you to have courage. This spell may be cast during any moon phase, but for best results, definitely work this herb magic on a Thursday, the day of the week named after this protective and powerful Norse god.

To begin, find a nice, healthy birch tree, and choose a six-inch length of red satin ribbon. Tie the ribbon loosely onto a low branch, and repeat the following charm:

> *The birch tree is sacred to the god Thor,*
> *Protect me now, keep bad luck from my door.*

Tie this red ribbon on, and the spell is begun,
As I will so mote it be, an let it harm none.

Whisper your thanks to the birch tree and to Thor, in your own words. Leave the ribbon, and turn and walk confidently home.

Garden Witchery: From Garden to Cauldron

My garden is run wild!
Where shall I plant anew—
For my bed, that once was covered with thyme,
Is all overrun with rue?

—MRS. FLEETWOOD HABERGHAM

Rue

Perennial rue *(Ruta graveolens)* has the planetary correspondence of Mars and is linked to the element of fire. Rue gets its name from the Latin word *ruta,* which means "bitterness" or "unpleasantness." On the other hand, the folk name for rue is the "herb of grace." This name came from the custom of sprinkling holy water from small branches of rue before religious services. Deity associations include Diana and her daughter, Aradia. Rue is a popular and frequently used herb in Italian Witchcraft, or *Stregheria.* In medieval times, rue was also one of the more potent disinfecting, strewing herbs.

In the garden, you will need to keep rue clipped back to a neat shape, and care should be taken if you have small children. Rue is toxic and an abortifacient. It may also cause contact dermatitis (a rash) if you have sensitive skin and brush up against the foliage. Use gardening gloves when you go to gather a stem or two, as the leaves are covered in oil glands. The scent is strong and bracing.

In herb magic, the rue plant breaks any hex, evil eye, curse, or manipulative magic. It's a protective plant, and when grown in the garden, it transforms the entire yard into a magical sanctuary. If you gather a little bundle and hang it indoors, it will ward the entire house. A fresh branch of rue was often used to sprinkle blessed water around a person or place to remove negativity and to perform a cleansing. This gorgeous blue-green plant grows into a miniature shrub in the sunny herb garden. Monarch caterpillars adore munching on it, and you will be rewarded with butterflies that enjoy the bright yellow blossoms. I grow rue in my herb gardens and enjoy its structure, color, and blossoms in the summertime.

Rue and Lavender Ritual for Transformation

In the opening of this chapter, I mentioned a clever Witch I know who transforms negative energy and situations and then puts that energy to positive use. Well, here is a ritual with an herb-magic spin on that idea.

In my mind, the difference between a charm, a spell, and a ritual is the length of time it takes you to perform them. A charm is quick, a spoken verse with few props. A spell is more involved and incorporates several items, such as candles, crystals, herbs, and color magic. A ritual is even more involved, and may require magic that needs to be performed over several days' time, plus the use of meticulous astrological timing. The magic itself simply takes longer to perform.

This herb magic falls into the "ritual" category. The ritual has several parts and takes seven days to complete. Any day of the week or moon phase may be used for this spell. Remember, what you are doing with this spell is manipulating negative energy and then transforming it into something positive. This requires visualization skills and a firm belief in yourself that you *can* do it. It is also important that you avoid beginning this ritual when the Moon is "void of course" or when the planet Mercury is retrograde. At these times, magical energy seems to go wonky anyway, so hedge your bets and steer clear of them. I recommend consulting a good astrological calendar before you cast this spell.

To begin, take a hard look at whatever negative situation you are facing, and keep the goal of transformation firmly in mind. You will need some fabric and ribbon or an organza favor bag to make your herbal charm bag. (You choose the colors. By this time you should have color magic down pat, anyway.) You will also need a white, seven-day jar candle, a few sprigs of rue, and a handful of lavender buds. Lavender is an herb of transformation, so it is just the ingredient to add to this herbal spell. You will also need a safe, flat surface to work on, and a lighter or some matches.

Set up your jar candle in a safe place where it can remain while burning. Pour the lavender buds into the charm bag, and then add the sprigs of rue. Tie the bag closed, and hold it in the palms of your hands. Take a moment to ground and center. Then visualize the transforming powers of lavender and the protective influence of rue swirling together and spinning out into the world to do their job. Know that you can turn whatever negative energy you are facing into a very positive situation. When you feel ready, repeat this spell verse three times:

> *Rue and lavender make a wonderful pair,*
> *As they bring protection and help clear the air.*
> *Now transform this situation, and spin it away,*
> *Bring good luck and positive change to all of my days.*

Set the charm bag aside, and go and light the seven-day candle. Repeat these lines:

> *With the power of herbs, this spell is begun,*
> *By the light of this candle, this spell is spun.*
> *I safely transform and change all negativity,*
> *For the good of all, as I will it, so mote it be!*

Allow the jar candle to burn in a safe place until it goes out on its own. (Try setting it inside an old metal pot or inside your cauldron. The bottom of a shower stall or kitchen sink works well too.) Now keep the herbal charm bag with you for the next seven days, or for as long as it takes for the candle to burn out. Each night before you retire for the evening, repeat the following lines:

> *Another day has passed, change is coming my way,*
> *Now good luck, protection, and peace, come home to stay.*

Once the candle has burned out, return the herbal ingredients neatly to nature, dispose of the empty candle jar, and then wash your hands. Take a deep breath, and go outside and face the sun. Tip your face up to the light, and take a moment to congratulate yourself on a job well done. Then close the ritual with this line:

> *By the power of herbs, this magic was spun,*
> *I close this now in peace, and brought harm to none.*

Lavender

Lavender (*Lavandula* ssp.) is aligned with the planet Mercury and the element of air. This aromatic, shrubby, tender perennial brings purification and peace. Lavender has been worked into various magics for thousands of years. The ancient Egyptians, Greeks, and Romans all used lavender. The Greeks and Romans used it most often as a bathing additive. This flowering herb was very popular in the Elizabethan era and was widely grown as a border plant in formal knot gardens. It was also a popular household fragrance for linens, and the herb was added to soaps and perfumes. The essential oil of lavender has antiseptic properties and has been used for centuries to treat scrapes and stings and to dress wounds.

Lavender promotes good luck when grown in the garden. An herb of transformation, lavender is also good for cleansings, restful sleep, and protection. The aroma of lavender is said to help relieve headaches and to encourage relaxation. Lavender was a common strewing herb, as it was believed to keep flies away and it helped hide unpleasant odors.

If you choose to grow lavender at home, make sure you buy a variety that is appropriate for your area. In my Zone 5 gardens, I have great success with Munstead lavender. Lavender is a drought-tolerant plant and will do well in a sunny, hot spot, such as along a sidewalk or driveway. If you snip back the spent blossoms (deadhead), this herb will keep producing those fabulously scented flowers throughout the growing season.

Lavender Sachet for Loving Protection

For this sachet, I suggest using a sheer organza bag, because you will want to see the lavender that is held within. I recommend the color purple, as it is a powerful magical color and it coordinates nicely with the lavender. Try a spice shop or even an arts and crafts store for packages of dried lavender buds. You will be using a good amount, and you don't want to strip the plants in your garden.

This sachet spell makes a lovely gift, or you can make one for yourself. It can be used as a traditional sachet and tucked into your dresser drawer to lightly scent your clothes. Pour a few handfuls of the lavender buds into the organza bag, and tuck a stem or two of fresh lavender from your magical garden in there as well. Tie it securely closed, and enchant the bag with the following protective charm:

> *In this purple bag a simple charm is contained,*
> *Bring protection and love to the person I name.*

Say the recipient's name out loud. Then say:

> *A gift from me to you, this loving charm I cast,*
> *May all your days be filled with joy that surely lasts.*

Now, give the lavender sachet bag as a gift, with your best wishes for a sweet, safe, and happy life.

Miracles do not happen in contradiction to nature,
but only in contradiction to what we know of nature.

—SAINT AUGUSTINE

CHAPTER SIX

HERB MAGIC FOR PROSPERITY

In this last theme chapter, we will study the topic of herbal prosperity magic. Working with items from nature is a commonsense approach to magic. If you incorporate herbs and natural items that you already have on hand, it will help you to save money, after all.

Also it is important to remember that the prosperity for which you are casting is not going to manifest itself as pound notes or dollar bills that just drop out of the sky. There is no such thing as a free lunch. The truth is that magic follows the path of least resistance. You are going to have to work toward increasing your prosperity. This may happen in many subtle ways. You may have the opportunity to work a little overtime, or to pick up a few extra hours at a part-time job. Or perhaps a new career opportunity will present itself, or you might find yourself up for a raise. Cast your herbal prosperity magic wisely, and remember that this type of magic works on the principle that there is a legitimate need here. A spell will manifest to answer your request and to meet that need, but it will probably not produce results if you're being greedy.

When casting spells for abundance and prosperity, work during a waxing moon or full moon to pull success toward you. In a pinch, you may cast these prosperity spells in a waning moon—just be sure to work for the removal of stress, money worries, despair, etc. (Remember, as the moon wanes, so do your cash-flow problems.) Then follow up during the next waxing moon to encourage the prosperity to flow toward you.

The most popular day of the week for casting money spells is a Thursday, Jupiter's day. This day has the correspondence of prosperity and wealth. The symbol for Jupiter looks like this: ♃. You can carve this into candles or stitch it onto charm bags for a little extra power. You can also cast your herbal prosperity spells on a Sunday, the Sun's day, which would pull the energies of abundance and success into your magic. The Sun's astrological symbol is ☉.

Prosperity magic is also aligned with the element of earth. The earth itself represents stability and abundance. As herb magic is an *earthy* magic, the positive energies are already there. All you have to do is tap into them, direct them, and then work those herbal spells and charms for your desired outcome.

Prosperity Spells from the Spice Rack

It's a funny thing about life;
if you refuse to accept anything but the best, you very often get it.
—WILLIAM SOMERSET MAUGHAM

Allspice

Allspice *(Pimento officinalis)* is linked to the planet Mars and the element of fire. This herb is the dried, unripe berry of the evergreen tree *Pimenta dioica*, which belongs to the myrtle family. The dried berries are a dark-brown color and small, just about the same size as peppercorns.

The history of allspice is a colorful one. Christopher Columbus discovered allspice in the Caribbean while searching for pepper. Old Columbus had never seen real pepper, and he thought that the allspice plant was what he'd been searching for. He brought the herb back to Spain, where it was called *pimenta*, the Spanish word for pepper. Today, allspice comes from Jamaica, Mexico, and Honduras.

Allspice is a common seasoning that is often used as a substitute for cinnamon. Nowadays, it is often found in the spice rack and is used as a pickling spice and to season pies and pastries. In herbalism, allspice is used to promote good luck and money. Some herbal texts claim that allspice promotes relief for nervous stomachs, promotes loving vibrations, and speeds healing too. Powdered allspice could even be burned as an incense on charcoal blocks to attract prosperity and to get your cash flowing. For a fast and practical herb magic, try the following charm.

Kitchen Witch Aromatherapy Charm

This practical little charm can be worked at any time or during any moon phase. Try adding a teaspoon of the powdered herb to a few cups of water in a tea kettle, and bring it to a boil on the stove. When the pot starts to steam, it will permeate the air with the wonderful scent and add a prosperous vibration to your home. Try this quick, Kitchen Witch–style charm as the wonderful scent begins to fill your kitchen:

> *By the power of fire and with this fragrant steam,*
> *Allspice will bring success and help me fulfill my dreams.*

Cinnamon

Cinnamon *(Cinnamomum zeylanicum)* has the planetary association of the Sun and is linked to the element of fire. This popular spice is associated with the goddess Venus/ Aphrodite. Both the ancient Egyptians and Romans used cinnamon, and it was considered a sacred and magical

Dinner 3
x egg roll
wonton soup

chicken [illegible scribble]

5195390130

herb. The Egyptians imported the herb from China, and it is thought that the search for cinnamon may have been the main reason for world exploration during the fifteenth and sixteenth centuries. Cinnamon is the dried bark of various laurel trees in the *Cinnamomum* family, such as the cassia tree. The cinnamon stick is actually long pieces of bark that are rolled, pressed, and dried.

Today, in the kitchen, cinnamon is added to fruit, cheese dishes, chicken, and lamb, and typically flavors pastries, pies, and cakes. Even folks who don't like to cook usually have powdered cinnamon in the cabinet. These days, most of the cinnamon we use comes from Asia and Central America.

Cinnamon is a handy magical herb to have around. It promotes psychic abilities, success, lust, love, and health. When cinnamon-scented incense is burned, or the actual spice is burned on charcoal blocks, it releases a money-drawing vibration into the air.

For magical purposes, you may work with powdered cinnamon or cinnamon sticks. I have found over the years that small cinnamon sticks are neater and easier to work magic with, but use what you have on hand. Add the fragrant sticks to charm bags and sachets that will pull success and prosperity your way.

Sundays Are for Success Charm Bag

For best results, try working this charm on a bright, sunny Sunday afternoon. Since cinnamon is associated with the Sun and fire, this would be your best bet. For this charm bag, the ingredients are simple. You'll need a few small cinnamon sticks and a dollar bill, plus a six-inch square of green fabric and coordinating ribbons to tie it closed, or a sheer organza favor bag in green. Roll up the dollar bill and then insert it and the cinnamon sticks inside the organza bag, or place them in the center of the fabric and gather up the edges. Tie the bag closed with three knots, saying:

By all the power of three times three,
As I will it, so shall it be.

Now, take the bag to a sunny window, or go outside, weather permitting. Stand in the sunshine for a few moments and hold the charm bag in the palms of your hands, allowing the sunlight to fall upon it. Feel the might and power of the sun soak into the bag and empower the herbs within. When you are ready, repeat this charm three times:

Cinnamon sticks do align with prosperity,
A little herb magic brings change quickly to me.
Empowered by the sun, for fortune and success,
May my prosperity charm bag be truly blessed.

Pocket the charm bag, or place it inside your briefcase or purse. Go about your business, and be assured that success and prosperity will come quickly into your life. If you decide to dismantle this charm bag at a later date, do not spend the dollar, but instead donate it to charity.

Ginger

Ginger *(Zingiber officinale)* has the planetary association of Mars and is linked to the element of fire. It was first grown by the Chinese and the Indians. The name actually comes from the Sanskrit word *sinabera*, which translates to "shaped like horns." Ginger is a native plant of tropical Asia and was used by the ancient Greeks and Romans. The Romans brought it to Britain, where it was grown carefully in medieval gardens but had to be harvested well before the first cold days of fall. The ginger perished quickly, root and all, at the first hint of cold temperatures.

Ginger root may be purchased whole, or you can find it dried, ground, or crystallized with sugar. Today, most of our ginger comes from India and Jamaica and gives breads and cookies a warm, comforting taste. Ginger root is back in vogue these days as a popular cooking spice. But if you don't care to work with the roots, the powdered ginger from the spice rack is easy to obtain and simple to work herb magic with. Try sprinkling some powdered ginger in your pockets to attract money into your life, or create an herbal sachet with pieces of ginger root to encourage prosperity and success.

Ginger Root Sachet

Try this spell on a Thursday, for abundance and prosperity, or a Sunday, for riches and success. Work in the waxing moon, to pull positive energies toward you, or the night of the full moon, for extra power. For this sachet, we will be incorporating one of the other featured herbal trees from this prosperity chapter—the oak tree. This charm bag not only helps improve your financial situation, but it also grants you the wisdom to help you manage your new prosperity.

You will need a handful of chopped ginger root (or a small piece), a silver coin, and one pretty leaf from an oak tree. As usual, the type of sachet bag you use is completely up to you. You can sew one up on a machine, tie the corners together from a square of fabric, or use a premade, sheer favor bag. Suggested colors for ribbons and fabrics would be green, silver, and gold.

Place the ginger, the coin, and the oak leaf inside the herbal sachet, and fasten it closed. Then repeat this charm three times:

> *Add a pinch of ginger root to a charm bag so green,*
> *It pulls money into your life and works like a dream.*
> *Add a silver coin for riches, and one oak leaf so fine,*
> *Now you'll be blessed with success and wisdom for all time.*

Close the spell as you wish, or use the tag line from chapter 1:

> *For the good of all, with harm to none.*
> *By herb magic this spell is done.*

Carry the sachet with you, in a pocket or purse, for one month. Then open the bag, save the silver coin for another time, and return the herbal contents to nature.

Oats

Oats *(Avena sativa)* are aligned with the planet Venus and the element of earth. Deities associated with this grain are Earth Mother goddesses and goddesses of the harvest. The cultivated oat plant and the wild oat *(Avena Fatua)* are described as annual plants with upright stems, bladelike leaves, and clusters of three florets that form the grain. The dried stems of the oat plant are called oatstraw. Oats are easy to digest and are good for you to boot. In the olden days, oats were fed to the livestock and were a staple food for people, as they were made into porridge, oatcakes, pastries, and, of course in modern times, breads, cakes, and cookies. Oatmeal, a very healthy and popular food these days, is rich in vitamin E, minerals, and protein. Plus, it's thought that eating a bowl of oatmeal every morning will help lower your cholesterol.

Oats are a great additive to the bath to relieve dry skin. Try adding a half cup of dry oatmeal to your bath water to soften and soothe itchy, dry skin. If you don't want loose oats going down the pipes, then stack up a couple of coffee filters, add a handful of oats to the center, and fasten it closed tightly with a rubber band. Toss the bundle in the water, and see how that works for you.

In herbalism, oats are often incorporated into money and prosperity spells. This grain can be a symbol for the Earth Mother and the Greco-Roman goddesses of the harvest, such as Demeter and Ceres. Best of all, you probably have some oatmeal in your pantry, and it is a nice, inexpensive ingredient to add to prosperity spells and sachets.

Harvest Goddess Spell for Abundance

This spell is a good one when you need to pull prosperity and abundance to your whole family. The goddesses in this spell are good to call on in this situation, as they have an affinity for working mothers, families, and loving parents.

You will need the following supplies:

- One plain, white tealight candle
- A straight pin or nail to engrave the astrological symbol of Ceres (♀) into the top of the candle
- A saucer
- A few tablespoons of dried oatmeal
- An image or symbol of Demeter/Ceres (the Mother card from the Tarot works well, or surf the Net and find a little picture to print out)
- A lighter or some matches
- A safe, flat surface to work on

Set the saucer on your work area, and place the tealight candle in the center of the saucer. With the pin or nail, carefully engrave the symbol for Ceres (♀) into the top of the candle, as neatly as you can. Sprinkle the dried oats in a circle around the tealight. (Keep the oats a few inches away from the candle, for safety's sake, but still on the saucer, for an easy cleanup.) Place the image of Demeter/Ceres off to the side of the plate.

Take a moment to focus your thoughts on the image of the Earth Mother and the Greco-Roman goddesses of the harvest. Ceres/Demeter was typically portrayed as a beautiful, full-figured, middle-aged woman wearing a blue robe. This goddess had golden hair that was braided and wrapped around her head, coronet style. Then light the candle, and repeat this charm three times:

The goddesses Ceres and Demeter I now call,
Send your abundance to this house, bless us one and all.
With this grain so simple and by candlelight,
Grant us your favor, on this enchanted night.

Allow the tealight candle to burn until it goes out on its own. (Typically, this takes about four hours.) After the candle is spent, neatly dispose of the little metal cup, and take the oats outside as an offering to the goddesses Ceres and Demeter. Put away the rest of your supplies, and set the image of the goddess in a prominent place for one week.

Enchanting Plants You May Not Know Are Herbs

He's in clover. In luck, in prosperous circumstances,
in a good situation.

—E. COBHAM BREWER, *DICTIONARY OF PHRASE AND FABLE*

Clover

Clover (*Trifolium* ssp.) is linked to the element of air. White clover corresponds to the planet Mercury, while red clover corresponds to Venus. During medieval times, clover was grown as a crop for animals, or cultivated as a "green manure" crop, which was then tilled back into the soil as compost. As it began to break down, it enriched the soil. Today, you can still try planting clover as green manure, but be aware that it will take a few seasons, because it's slow to establish itself. For best results, it needs a year or two of growing before you till it under.

The clover flowers were made into wine, and were especially important to beekeepers, as the clover nectar was made into superior-tasting honey. They are also prized by children, who enjoy picking them and making a flower chain out of them for good luck.

The clover, just as you would imagine, is used in herbalism to promote good luck, wealth, and success. The charming clover may also be used to predict a coming shower. If you find that the clovers leaves are folded up tight one summer morning, then you should expect rain to fall that very afternoon. The clover closes up its leaves in the evening hours, so if you want to try to predict the weather, check it out in the morning hours. When clover grows wild in your yard, you have been blessed by the Fae, and this happy little plant will help keep negativity at bay and snakes away from your property.

The white clover flower was utilized in hex-breaking and to ward off negativity, while the red clover was believed to promote lust and to assist in financial dealings of every kind. Adding clover flowers and foliage to charm bags and herbal sachets that you make as gifts brings good luck and cheerfulness to the recipient.

Clover typically is found growing as three leaves, which can be a symbol for the triple goddesses, such as the Celtic Brigid, and for all magical trinities, such as the Maiden, Mother, and Crone, or the Mother, Father, and Child. However, the different numbers of leaves that are possible on the clover have separate magical meanings:

Three leaves—The three-leaf clover represents eternity and the trinity. The trefoil is worn as a shielding talisman or charm and also to promote prosperity and good fortune. Placing a three-leaf clover in your shoe grants visions of the faeries.

Four leaves—The four-leaf clover signifies harmony and the four quarters of the magic circle. It is especially lucky. It was believed to protect you from melancholy, allow you to sense the presence of ghosts, and strengthen your psychic abilities. If a four-leaf clover was tucked into your shoe, you were sure to meet a new love. It was also thought to lead its bearer to hidden treasures or that elusive pot o' gold. Press a four-leaf clover in your Book of Shadows for an herbal book blessing.

Five leaves—The rare five-leaf clover symbolizes fame and fortune, and is thought to attract cash and riches.

Six leaves—The six-leaf clover conveys wealth and treasures. Since there are double the number the leaves, imagine that this uncommon clover brings double the magical *oomph* of the traditional three leaves.

Seven leaves—The seven-leaf clover traditionally brings to its bearer long, happy years filled with riches and joy.

Lucky Clover Spell

Well, you should know this by heart now: Cast this spell on a Thursday, for abundance and prosperity, or a Sunday, for riches and success. Cast during a waxing moon, to increase your good luck, and a waning moon, to banish bad luck. This herb and candle spell is pretty straightforward. If you have trouble finding silver-colored spell candles, then substitute with white tapers, tealights, votives, or even plain birthday candles. So don't panic—just use white (the all-purpose color) or even green candles for luck instead. You can always figure a way to work things out. Clever magic users remember to improvise, adapt, and overcome! Here is the supply list:

- 3 silver mini spell candles or votives
- 3 coordinating candle holders
- 3 three-leaf clovers
- A safe, flat surface to work on
- A lighter or some matches

Arrange the clovers between the candles, or as you prefer. Take a moment to ground and center yourself and visualize the trinity, however you see them. Lay your hands on the clovers, and make a silent request in your own words to be granted a bit of good luck. Now light the candles, and repeat this charm:

> *Three silver candles burning so bright,*
> *Bring good fortune to me on this night.*
> *The trefoil pattern of the clover leaves,*
> *Pulls prosperity and luck, straight to me.*
> *By the power of earth and fire, this charm is spun,*
> *As I will it, so shall it be, and let it harm none.*

Allow the candles to burn out in a safe place, but do not leave them unattended. Once they are consumed, tuck one of the clovers into your wallet, and the other two in your shoes. Now, good luck will stroll right into your life and into your pocketbook without any difficulties.

Periwinkle

Known as lesser periwinkle *(Vinca minor)* or greater periwinkle *(Vinca major)*, this perennial ground cover is associated with the planet Venus and the element of water. It is interesting to note that most plants with blue flowers are linked to the goddess Venus/Aphrodite. This flowering herb is a symbol of immortality. Historically, it was a popular motif for illuminated designs and floral engravings. Sometimes this plant is known as the "flower of death," due to its habit of growing all over graves at cemeteries. Keep in mind that periwinkle is toxic.

The lesser periwinkle is a common ground cover that is an evergreen springtime bloomer. The blossoms have five purple petals with white stars in the center, which no doubt helped the flower earn its name of "sorcerer's violet" and its reputation as a magical plant.

Try growing this ground cover in shady areas of your garden. Gather a few stems of this powerful herb, and keep it with you in your pocket to attract success and riches into your life.

Protecting Your Prosperity and Possessions

Well, sure, this topic belongs in a prosperity chapter. It costs money to replace stolen items or to repair damage from vandalism or from kids causing malicious mischief.

About a decade ago, my neighborhood had a problem with this type of scenario. Now while the items that were stolen from me weren't especially valuable, it was still aggravating. After all, I wouldn't have them on my house or in the yard if I didn't enjoy them. And the bottom line is it did cost me *more* money to replace them. So being a practical Witch, I decided to use one of the most powerful, multipurpose herbs in my garden to protect my possessions and to put an end to the neighborhood vandalism problem. I used the periwinkle. What follows is the spell that I used.

Periwinkle Witch Jar

The best time to work this spell is during the waning moon. You will need one clean, glass jar with a lid. Into this jar, place some periwinkle vines and foliage from the garden, and a photo of your residence or a piece of paper with your address written on it. Add a pinch of salt, to break up negativity, and a tablespoon of dried vervain, to make the spell move quickly. If you can't get your hands on vervain, then add some fresh rose petals to speed the spell on its way.

Screw the lid on the jar, and then, using a permanent black marker, draw on the top of the jar a five-pointed, upright star surrounded by a circle. (This symbol of positive magic is known as the pentacle.) Hold the sealed jar in both hands, and load it up with your intentions. Visualize what you wish it to do: protect your property and belongings and help catch the troublemakers. Then repeat this charm three times:

> *The sorcerer's violet bears a tiny white star,*
> *I tap into your power, placed into this jar.*
> *Now protect my possessions, and guard well my home,*
> *The vandal's fun is over, no more will they roam.*

Now, you have a couple options to finish the spell. You can tuck the jar inside your home, out of sight, in a room that sees a lot of traffic, like the living room or kitchen. Or, you can set it next to your front porch, behind the shrubs, or in the garden somewhere inconspicuous. Once you put the jar in place, close the spell with these lines:

Witch's jar, guard and protect my property,
Keep safe all my possessions, most carefully.

Keep the jar in place until the problem is solved. If things are really bad, add a few protection spells (from the previous chapter) to your home, while you're at it.

Honeysuckle

Honeysuckle (*Lonicera* ssp.), classified as a semievergreen plant, is neatly aligned with the planet Jupiter and the element of earth. Both of these magical associations are famous for increasing prosperity. Honeysuckle grows wild in many climates, and has been cultivated in gardens for its fragrance and to help draw honeybees. Its old folk name "woodbine" refers to the plant's tendency to wrap its tendrils around neighboring trees and shrubs.

A popular plant in antique illuminated designs and engravings, honeysuckle was named for the sweet taste of the nectar from the flowers. The berries of the honeysuckle are toxic, so please leave them alone, but the blossoms are lovely and make an enchanting addition to the landscape.

According to herbal tradition, honeysuckle promotes prosperity if grown near the house. Bringing the blooming branches into the house was believed to cause a wedding to occur. Working with fresh honeysuckle flowers also increases your chances of getting that dream job you've been after. Another fun bit of herbal trivia says that if the blossoms are set in a girl's room, they will encourage dreams of her future husband.

Today, the flowers are worked into perfumes and are often added to potpourri mixes. The shrub is grown in the garden to encourage good luck and to encourage the presence of those all-important pollinating insects, such as butterflies and bees.

Get a New Job with Honeysuckle

So you've been pounding the pavement, looking for a new or better job? Good for you! Now that you've turned in your applications, perhaps you'd like to sweeten your chances of being called back for an interview. Or perhaps you are waiting to hear an offer after the interview. Well, this beautiful herbal spell should help.

This spell would work well on a Thursday (Jupiter's day) and during a waxing or full moon. Here is the supply list:

- A business card or letterhead of the place where you have applied
- A handful of honeysuckle blossoms
- 4 green votive candles for prosperity, good luck, a new job, and fresh beginnings
- 4 accompanying votive-candle cup holders
- A straight pin or nail to engrave the candles
- A lighter or some matches
- A safe, flat surface to work on

(Please note: Votives immediately turn to liquid wax as they burn, so you should always burn them inside votive cups. If you don't, you'll have a big puddle of wax all over your work area.)

To begin, carefully engrave a dollar symbol (or a symbol of whatever currency is used where you live) on the side of the first green candle. On the second candle, engrave a three-leaf clover for good luck. On the third candle, engrave the words "new job." Finally, on the fourth candle, engrave a waxing crescent moon (☽) to symbolize those fresh beginnings. Now place all the votive candles into their candle cups. Set the business card/letterhead flat on your work surface, in front of the candles. Take a moment or two to center yourself. Then light the candles and repeat this spell:

> *Four magic green candles that burn away,*
> *Help me bring prosperous change my way.*
> *One candle for money, another for good fortune,*
> *A third for my new career, may I obtain it soon.*
> *The fourth candle bears the symbol of the waxing moon,*
> *May the job be offered to me, hear this Witch's tune.*

At this point, arrange the honeysuckle blossoms around the bases of the candles. Just be sure to keep the flowers and your fingers well away from the flames. Close the spell with these lines:

> *Honeysuckle blooms, with your scent so sweet,*
> *grant my request with all possible speed.*

Allow the candles to burn until they go out on their own. (Votive candles take approximately six to eight hours to burn away.) When the candles are gone, clean up your work area and keep the blossoms until they start to fade. Allow the flowers to air-dry and then tuck them, along with the business card or folded letterhead, into charm bags or herbal sachets that you can carry with you for continued good luck when you start your new job.

Herbal Trees for Abundance and Success

Sweet is the whispering music of yonder pine that sings.

—THEOCRITUS

Pine

The pine tree (*Pinus* ssp.), classified as a coniferous evergreen, is associated with the planet Mars and the element of air. It comes in dozens of varieties and is extremely long-lived. This multipurpose tree was sacred to many gods and goddesses, such as Pan, Venus, Dionysus, Bacchus, and Astarte. It was considered magical, as it kept its luxurious green color all year long and represented life in the darkest, coldest days of the year. Is it any wonder that the pine became synonymous with the rebirth of the sun god at the winter solstice? This herbal evergreen tree was valued for its wood, resin, and tar.

Hanging fresh-cut boughs in the home, and over doorways at the winter solstice, was believed to bring good fortune and prosperity to all who lived in the home. The fruit of the pine tree, the pine cone, is considered to be a phallic symbol that represents abundance, new life, and fertility. If you enjoy collecting pine cones and displaying them in baskets or bowls, you can try charming them to increase the prosperity for your entire household.

The supple green needles of the pine may be tucked into sachets and charm bags to promote prosperity and fortune. Fresh, fragrant pine needles may be scattered throughout the house to drive away negativity and to naturally freshen the air. And here's another practical, magical aromatherapy tip: green, pine-scented candles promote prosperity too. Light one tonight, and try a quick prosperity charm over it. Here's a good one.

Pine Spell for Prosperity

Work this spell on a Thursday, and during a waxing moon, to pull abundance toward you, or during a waning moon, to remove worries and fears over financial situations. Light a green, pine-scented candle, and repeat this spell:

> *Bless this scented spell candle that burns so bright,*
> *Send prosperity and abundance tonight.*

If you want to jazz up this little spell, you could engrave a dollar symbol or the astrological symbol for Jupiter (♃) on the side of the candle. Lastly, try arranging a few snips of fresh pine at the base of the spell candle. Happy casting!

Oak

The deciduous oak tree (*Quercus* ssp.) is associated with the planet Jupiter and the element of fire. A solar tree that is also associated with thunder and lightning, this tree is sacred to many religions and cultures. It is associated with the gods Thor, Jupiter, and Zeus. This long-lived tree can grow up to 150 feet in height and is often used as a sentinel or a marker of a sacred and magical place. Many magical rituals were held under the spreading branches of the oak. Some people believe that the word *Druid* comes from the old Gaelic word *duir*, which translates to "men of the oak" or even "oak knowledge." Herbal tradition states that if you wear a chaplet or crown of oak leaves while calling on any of these gods, your petition will receive special notice.

The oak tree has links to each of the sabbats, and thus is a powerful symbol for the wheel of the year. You could create an amulet for protection by tying two oak twigs together, following the directions for creating a solar amulet out of ash that was featured previously (see "Herbal Sachet for Healing" in chapter 4). It is said that holding a green oak leaf to your heart and asking a question out loud to the spirit of the oak tree will soon show you the truth in any matter.

The fruit of the oak tree, the acorn, was once used as a food source in ancient times. Acorns were also fed to the livestock. The little acorn is a powerful talisman for good health and fertility, and also to increase a man's sexual prowess and to promote prosperity. It is also a miniature symbol for the potency and life-giving power of the God. In herb magic, you can try planting an acorn in the waning moon to receive money in the future. Another fun idea is to create a pocket charm with a trio of acorns, and keep them in your pocket to increase your prosperity.

Acorn Pocket Charm for Prosperity

This pocket charm is quick and easy to make. First, go take a walk around the neighborhood or to the local park, and find an oak tree. Take a look on the ground beneath the tree. Gather a trio of nice acorns, and take them home with you. Once you get them home, hold them in your hands and imagine that they are surrounded with a bright, green light. Then enchant them with the following charm:

From little acorns mighty oaks grow, they say,
These charming talismans, send success my way.
Bring to me prosperity with the charm I rhyme,
This spell will create abundance, come rain or shine.

Slip the enchanted acorns in your pocket, and off you go.

Garden Witchery: From Garden to Cauldron

A garden full of sweet odours is a garden full of charm.
—LOUISE BEEBE WILDER, *THE FRAGRANT GARDEN*

Heliotrope

Heliotrope *(Heliotropium arborescens)* has the planetary correspondence of the Sun and the elemental association of fire. This fragrant blooming herb is a favorite of mine and will thrive in a sunny area of your garden. Heliotrope grows into a little shrub by the end of the fall, and if you keep its spent flower heads clipped off (a process called deadheading), it will continue to bloom all summer long. Heliotrope is listed as a toxic plant, so keep it away from youngsters. This herb gets its name from *Helios*, the Greek god of the sun, and the Greek word *trope*, which means "to turn." It was thought that the blossoms turned to face the sun throughout the day.

This herb makes masses of purple flowers that have a wonderful cherry-vanilla scent, which is how it earned its folk name "cherry pie." (There are some white blooming varieties too.) The dark-purple blossoms add a lot of visual impact to your garden. Keep in mind that the foliage of heliotrope may cause mild skin irritations, such as a prickly, red rash, so wear gloves while handling this herb.

In herb magic, you can put these sweet-smelling flowers in a sachet bag, and tuck it into your pocket to attract money. You can also place the flowers in a circle around a gold or purple candle to draw prosperity.

Sunny Spell with Heliotrope

This spell is a flower fascination, with candle magic to add some power. But here's where we mix things up a bit. You should have the basic correspondences down by now, but I don't want you to get stuck in a rut with green, Thursday, Jupiter, and blah, blah, blah.

So check this out. Purple is also a color associated with the planet Jupiter. The mystical color purple brings spirituality and power to magical workings, and is a very popular color among magic users. The gold candle is a symbol for the Greek god of the sun, Helios, and of course heliotrope was named after Helios. Helios brings victory, change, and riches into your life, so he's a good deity to work with in prosperity spells. In this spell, you will call on him to bring success shining into your life. And, if you remember, gold is a color of the sun, and the sun promotes success, riches, and fame.

Here are the supplies you will need:

- 2 purple candles, for magical power
- 1 gold candle, to represent the sun god Helios
- 3 coordinating candle holders
- A straight pin or nail to engrave the candles
- Fresh heliotrope blossoms
- A lighter or some matches
- A safe, flat surface to work on

Work this spell on a Sunday, the day of the week that was once named after Helios. (The Greeks called this day *hermera heliou.*) If you can, set up this spell in a spot where the sunshine can beam down on your work area.

Position your candles with the gold in the center and the purple candles flanking it on either side. Carve a Sun symbol ($\odot$) into the center of the gold candle, and turn it so the engraving faces you. Arrange the heliotrope blossoms around the candles, and take a moment to enjoy their cherry scent. Think about what it is you really need to work for—nah, not millions of dollars, but to be a happy and prosperous person.

Put yourself in a positive frame of mind. Then light the candles, and repeat this spell:

> *Heliotrope has the folk name of cherry pie,*
> *I cast this spell today, under a sunny sky.*
> *The flowers circle the candles of purple and gold,*
> *If you want abundance and change, then you must be bold.*
> *I call on the sun god Helios, for drive and success,*
> *My hopes and dreams for prosperity, he will surely bless.*

Allow the candles to burn until they go out on their own. When the candles are consumed, clean up your work area and then set the heliotrope on a drying rack and allow the blossoms to air-dry. You may save these enchanted flowers to use for other prosperity charms in the future.

Cinquefoil

Cinquefoil *(Potentilla anserina)* has the planetary association of Jupiter and is aligned with the element of earth. This blooming perennial is a sun-loving herb that grows to about eighteen inches in height and is blessed with many folk names. One of the more popular ones is "five-finger grass." Each point of the leaf represents a different magical quality: wealth, well-being, power, love, and wisdom.

This herb has tiny yellow flowers from May through early fall. There are other varieties of cinquefoil, with different colors of blossoms. I have a variety named 'Miss Willmot,' and the blossoms are larger than most other varieties, and are a gorgeous coral color, but the bloom cycle lasts for only three weeks. The rest of the year, I simply enjoy the neat mounds of foliage.

Herbal lore recommends gathering this herb during the waxing moon and at midnight—how mysterious! Gather this herb whenever your schedule permits; it will work out fine no matter when you harvest it. The best thing about this plant is that when you incorporate it into any spell, it adds those five wonderful qualities of wealth, well-being, power, love, and wisdom to the magic.

Cinquefoil Charm

Do you want to add a little extra something to your herb magic? Well, here you go. This is a perfect herb to add. Just consider all of those positive magical correspondences for it, which were just listed. Try this herbal charm whenever you work with the cinquefoil. You could even add this as a tag line to herbal enchantments of your own design:

Five-finger grass can bring many good things to your life,
Wealth, health, power, love, and wisdom, without any strife.
Add this versatile herb, and the spell is begun,
As I will, so mote it be, and let it harm none!

Mint

Mint (*Mentha* ssp.) is a fragrant, perennial herb that is associated with the planets Venus, Pluto, and Mercury. Its elemental association is air. This fast-spreading and easy-to-grow herb was cultivated by the ancient Egyptians, Romans, and Greeks. It was also a popular herb in monastic gardens. The mint plant is associated with the Greek goddess Hecate and the god Hades, lord of the underworld.

Hades was known to the Romans as Pluto, so you can see how the planet Pluto became associated with this herb. According to legend, Hades/Pluto rarely left his underground kingdom, but on one such occasion he happened to meet a beautiful nymph named Minthe. Minthe and Hades shared a mutual attraction, but Hades' wife, Persephone, caught wind of Hades' infatuation, and before things could go any further, she changed Minthe into this sweet-smelling plant. Hecate, goddess of Witches, is also aligned with the mint plant.

Mint has a colorful reputation and is a multipurpose Witch plant. It's a popular magical herb for many different types of enchantments and charms. It's also famous for freshening breath and settling sour stomachs. Mint was also considered an aphrodisiac, and was often utilized as a strewing herb. Brides wore chaplets of this herb to bring good luck to their marriage. Mint was used in butcher shops to help keep flies away from the meat, and has been used as a culinary herb since ancient times. It flavored just about every kind of dish, including meats, fruits, confections, and beverages.

According to herbal folklore, growing mint in your garden is a sure-fire way to attract money into your purse. This is a type of sympathetic magic, as there is an old saying that wishes for "your money to be as plentiful as the mint leaves in the herb garden." You can also tuck a few sweet-smelling leaves in your wallet or handbag to pull prosperity to you.

Here is a down-to-earth spell to enchant the mint in your garden. This will bless your entire household with good luck, prosperity, and happiness.

Garden Witch Spell for Success and Prosperity

I recommend keeping this invasive herb in its own a container, or controlling its growth by tucking your new plant in a larger, soil-filled container and then sinking the container into the garden. Otherwise, the roots will shoot out, and it will spread everywhere.

You can work this spell anytime. It can be worked with the mint already growing in your garden, or you can perform this when you go to add a new mint plant in with your other herbs.

Take a seat on the ground, and run your hands over the fragrant mint leaves. Hold your hands to your face, and breathe in the refreshing scent. Then repeat this spell three times:

All around me, prosperity now quickly grows,
Magic is found in the earth, as a Witch surely knows.
May success bloom in my life in a positive way,
My life is magically blessed, each and every day.

Remember, magic is intention, and magic is love. It is the art of creating positive change. So get in there and see what amazing things you can accomplish. Cast your spells, and use your imagination to adapt and personalize the herbal enchantments featured in this book for love, health, happiness, success, and abundance. Brightest blessings and best wishes on all your herb craft!

Writing is an exploration.
You start from nothing and learn as you go.

—E. L. DOCTOROW

CHAPTER SEVEN

WRITING YOUR OWN HERBAL SPELLS AND CHARMS

In this, our last chapter, we are going to discuss a few more important topics. I don't want to just explain how herb magic works, show you the spells, and then turn you loose. I'd like to follow up with a few basics, so you feel confident as you take your next steps down this herbal path.

So, I imagine you are feeling pretty proud of yourself by now, as well you should. Together we have covered quite a bit of herb magic, and you are ready to put your own personalized spin on herbalism. There are a few more things you will need to help you in this venture, and they won't cost you a dime. What are they? Creativity, intuition, and imagination. Acquire these, and you will be ready to start experimenting and writing your own herbal spells and charms.

In truth, a spell is a mental projection for positive change that can performed in many ways. It may be cast spontaneously (when you envision a change, and it becomes so). A spell can be spoken aloud, in a divine sort of improvisation. Or it can be plotted out and written down.

If you are wondering where to begin and how to spark your own creativity when it comes time to set pen to paper, or fingers to keyboard, I have a few suggestions.

To Rhyme or Not to Rhyme?

If you'd like your herbal spells to rhyme but have a little trouble with that, go and purchase a rhyming dictionary. I keep one above my desk, with my reference books, and it often saves the day when I'm stuck on a spell verse. These little dictionaries are inexpensive, and easy and *fun* to use. Traditionally, the reason spells often rhyme is because a spell is a ritual, of sorts. There is an old adage that says that in order to make a spell powerful, you should make it rhyme. Here is my adaptation of that saying:

To empower your herb magic every time,
Let the charms and spells be spoken in rhyme.

This tradition goes along with the theory that repeating rhyming lines, while spellcasting, puts you in a different mental state, one that is more advantageous to working magic. Try it out for yourself and see how it works. Write one spell that doesn't rhyme and one that does, cast them both, and see which one has the better results.

If the very thought of trying to write rhyming spell verses, even with the help of a dictionary, makes you break a sweat, then take the pressure off yourself and don't worry about whether your verses rhyme. The world will not stop spinning if they don't. Try drafting a few simple spells that sound like you. If you can't imagine yourself reading the verses out loud with a straight face, then you've got a problem. Keep the spells and charms simple, and enjoy the creative process. The verses don't have to be grandiose and theatrical, okay?

On the other hand, if theatrical *is* your style, well then, hey, go for it.

More Ideas to Spark Your Creativity

Idea 1

Do something *else* creative. Yup, believe it or not, doing something artsy that you enjoy—whether it's knitting, woodworking, gardening, floral design, painting, or scrapbooking—can often take your mind off what you are stuck on, and get those creative juices flowing. There is something about using your hands to create something beautiful that puts you in a different state of mind. You become so focused on one project that your mind takes a break. Once you have finished the project, you often will find that when you go back to writing your herb spells, the writing part becomes easier. The thoughts and ideas just flow better.

Idea 2

Hit the books or take a class. Visit the local library. Check out a few big coffee-table type of books full of beautiful, color pictures of herbs and herb gardens, and see what inspires you. Go to an herb sale, or attend an herb society meeting. Sign up for a garden lecture, or take a gardening class. Check with your local university extension office, the local chapter of Master Gardener volunteers, or the nurseries in your area for classes.

Idea 3

Talk to other folks who are passionate about plants and herbs. All gardeners love to swap plants and care tips and share information. Besides, serious gardeners are a riot. Where else will you find so many different kinds of people who all act like kids at a bakery-store window when they come across green plants? The majority of gardeners that I know are earthy, generous, and practical, and they love to talk and pass information and plants along to others.

Idea 4

Get a change of scenery. Take a stroll through a nursery, park, or botanical garden armed with a notebook and a pen. See which herbs, trees, or plants capture your imagination. Perhaps you'll wander through a park in high summer and admire the roses, bend over to take a good whiff of their scent, and have a seat on a nearby bench and study them for a time. Getting any ideas? Is there a particular color you seemed to be drawn to? Well, whip that notebook out and take some notes. Take a few moments to write down your impressions, your emotions, and things you noticed about the plant. Later, back at home, leaf through your magical books, and see what other information and folklore you can add to your notes. Then sit down and see what sort of spell you can create, of your very own making.

Putting It on Paper

When I draft my own spells and charms, I have found it easiest to work from a worksheet. Here is one for you to copy and use. It is a wonderful tool to help you organize your supplies, calculate lunar and astrological timing, draft your spell verses, and plot out your best course of magical action.

Herbal Spell Worksheet

Goal: _____

_____

_____

_____

Moon phase: _____

Day of the week: _____

Astrological/magical symbols used: _____

_____

_____

_____

Herbs used: _____

_____

_____

_____

Magical significance of the herbs: _____

_____

_____

_____

Candle color (if you added candle magic): _____

_____

_____

_____

Fresh foliage or garden flowers: _____

_____

_____

_____

_____

Charm or verse: _____

_____

_____

_____

_____

_____

_____

_____

_____

_____

_____

_____

_____

_____

_____

Results: _____

_____

_____

_____

_____

_____

_____

_____

_____

_____

_____

_____

_____

_____

_____

_____

Keeping Track of Your Herb Magic

Learning is a treasure that accompanies its owner everywhere.
—CHINESE PROVERB

The "results" section at the bottom of the spell worksheet has a couple of purposes. First, this is an affirmation and a record of how your herb magic blossomed. It's very satisfying to look back and see how your magic worked. It will boost your confidence, and it's a great way to keep track of your results. It truly does help to write down the outcomes of your herbal spells, so you have a record of what worked well and what did not.

Second, this is a solid way to learn as you go—the old trial and error method. Yes, sometimes spells flop, or turn out in a way you had not planned or could not possibly have imagined. So, keeping records of your herbal spells is a wonderful way to note your successes and learn from your failures. You can compare your spell notes, and then fine-tune your own herb magic, spells, and charms in the future.

So, live on the edge, and go pick up a spiral notebook and keep a record of your research and spellwork. Dare to study the basics. Get in there and adapt some charms, and try your hand at writing your own herb magic. Commit some herbal and magical knowledge to memory, and then create and cast spells and herb magics of your own creation. In truth, this is how you become a more advanced magical practitioner.

Memorize those daily correspondences from chapter 2. Trust me, you will use those planetary, color, and magical associations *every* time you cast *any* type of spell. If it will help, you can record all of this basic information in your notebook, and turn it into your magical journal, or what is often called a Book of Shadows.

If you don't already have a magical journal, there is no time like the present to begin one. Your personal magical journal, or Book of Shadows, is the place to write down your hopes and dreams, and what's on your mind. You can write down ideas you have for spells, or create a list of your favorite herbs, and so on. In time, it will become a treasured record of personal history. One day in the future, you'll look back on it and be amazed at yourself and how much you've grown as a magical herbalist.

After all, my first herb magic journal inspired me to write this book. I certainly never planned it that way, all those years ago. Taking a look back at my roots, at how I began as a Witch and where I came from, offered me a way to help other folks begin their own study of magical herbs.

Closing Thoughts: A Soul Garden

*The garden must be prepared in the soul first
or else it will not flourish.*

—ENGLISH GARDENING PROVERB

Enjoy your time in the natural world, working with herbs and plants. Rejoice in the connection you feel to the earth and her charming cycles and seasons. Think of your studies of magical herbalism as time spent in the soul's garden, because magic comes naturally in the garden. Whether your spiritual garden is found in pots and containers on a porch, tucked in jars of dried herbs in the kitchen cabinet, or growing in a large backyard herb bed, it really doesn't matter.

In the soul's garden, surrounded by magical plants and enchanting herbs, it's easy to feel the spiritual connection and life force inherent in all of nature. Awaken your senses and see what you can discover while working with herbs and all their fascinating properties and enchanting energies. Create your own herbal spells and charms with humor, style, and heart.

Believe in yourself, work your herb magic for positive change, for the best of all, and you will accomplish wonders.

HERBAL CORRESPONDENCES AND SUBSTITUTIONS

Here are a few more herb magic correspondence lists for you to refer to. You will notice that there are many herbs here that were not listed in the previous theme chapters.

Please note that these lists are not all-inclusive. There are many other herbs associated with the planets and elements as well. However, all of the following magical herbs are easy to find and practical to use in your own herbal spells and charms.

These herbs are not intended to be taken internally or to treat medical issues. Some are toxic. This listing is for charms and spells only.

Practical Elemental Herbs

Earth

    Barley

    Buckwheat

    Corn

    Cypress tree

    Ferns

    Honesty

    Honeysuckle

    Magnolia

    Mugwort (avoid during pregnancy)

    Oats

    Primrose

    Tulip

    Vervain

    Wheat

Air

    Almond

    Anise

    Aspen tree

    Borage

    Chicory

    Clover

    Dandelion

    Lavender

    Lemon grass

    Lemon verbena

Mace

Maple tree

Marjoram

Mint

Orange bergamot

Parsley

Pine tree (common allergen)

Sage

Witch hazel

Fire

Allspice

Angelica

Ash tree

Basil

Bay

Carnation

Cedar tree

Chili pepper (keep away from eyes)

Cinnamon

Clove

Coneflower

Coriander

Dill

Fennel

Garlic

Ginger

Hawthorn tree

Heliotrope (may cause contact dermatitis)

Holly

Hyssop

Marigold

Mullein

Mustard

Oak

Orange

Pepper

Rosemary

Rowan tree (Mountain ash)

Rue (toxic; avoid handling during pregnancy)

St. John's wort

Snapdragon

Sunflower

Sweet woodruff

Thistle

Walnut (common allergen)

Water

African violet

Aloe

Apple

Birch tree

Catnip

Chamomile

Comfrey

Elder tree and berries

Elm tree

Eucalyptus (common allergen)

Feverfew

Gardenia

Heather

Iris

Jasmine

Lady's mantle

Lemon balm

Mallow

Pansy

Periwinkle (toxic)

Poplar tree

Raspberry

Rose

Spearmint

Strawberry (common allergen)

Sweet pea

Tansy

Vanilla

Violet

Wintergreen

Yarrow (may cause contact dermatitis; avoid during pregnancy)

Practical Planetary/Astrological Herbs

These herbs are not intended to be taken internally or to treat medical issues. Some are toxic. This listing is for charms and spells only.

Sun (Sunday)

Angelica

Ash tree

Bay

Carnation

Cedar

Chamomile

Chrysanthemum

Cinnamon

Heliotrope (may cause contact dermatitis)

Juniper

Marigold

Oak

Orange

Peony

Rosemary

Rowan tree

Rue (toxic; avoid handling during pregnancy)

St. John's wort

Sunflower

Witch hazel

Moon (Monday)

Aloe

Eucalyptus (common allergen)

Gardenia

Grape

Honesty

Jasmine

Lemon

Loosestrife

Mallow

Moonflower (mildly toxic)

Poppy

Pumpkin

Sandalwood

Willow

Wintergreen

Mars (Tuesday)

Allspice

Basil

Chili pepper (keep away from eyes)

Coriander

Dragon's blood resin

Garlic

Ginger

Hawthorn tree

Holly

Mustard

Nettle

Onion

Pepper

Peppermint

Pine tree (common allergen)

Snapdragon

Sweet woodruff

Thistle

Yucca

Mercury (Wednesday)

Almond

Aspen tree

Celery seed

Clover

Dill

Fennel

Fern

Horehound

Lavender

Lemon grass

Mace

Marjoram

Mint

Parsley

Pomegranate

Jupiter (Thursday)

Anise

Betony

Borage

Cinquefoil

Clove

Dandelion

Honeysuckle

Hyssop

Linden tree

Maple tree

Meadowsweet

Nutmeg

Oak tree

Sage

Venus (Friday)

Apple

Aster

Banana

Barley

Birch tree

Blackberry

Catnip

Cherry

Columbine

Elder tree

Feverfew

Foxglove (toxic)

Geranium

Heather

Iris

Lady's mantle

Lilac

Magnolia

Oats

Orchid

Periwinkle (toxic)

Primrose

Raspberry

Rose

Spearmint

Strawberry (common allergen)

Tansy

Thyme

Valerian

Vanilla

Vervain

Violet

Wheat

Willow

Saturn (Saturday)

Amaranth (Love-lies-bleeding)

Beech tree

Belladonna (toxic)

Comfrey

Cypress tree

Elm

Hellebore (toxic)

Ivy (berries are toxic)

Lobelia

Mimosa

Morning glory (mildly toxic)

Mullein

Pansy

Patchouli

Poplar tree

Quince

Slippery elm

Yew (toxic)

Featured Herbs for Love and Happiness

Basil

Chili pepper (keep away from eyes)

Columbine

Maple tree

Marjoram

Rose

Rosemary

Strawberry (common allergen)

Thyme

Vanilla bean

Violet

Willow tree

Yarrow (may cause contact dermatitis; avoid during
 pregnancy)

Featured Herbs for Well-Being and Comfort

Ash tree

Chamomile

Coriander

Dianthus

Feverfew

Lady's mantle

Mace

Nutmeg

Parsley

Purple coneflower

Sage

Witch hazel

Featured Herbs for Protection

Anise

Bay leaf

Birch tree

Calendula (Pot marigold)

Dill

Elder tree

Garlic

Holly

Lamb's ears

Lavender

Rue (toxic; avoid handling during pregnancy)

Featured Herbs for Prosperity

Allspice

Cinnamon

Cinquefoil

Clover

Ginger

Heliotrope (may cause contact dermatitis)

Honeysuckle

Mint

Oak tree

Oats

Periwinkle (toxic)

Pine tree (common allergen)

Emergency Herb Magic Substitutions

If an herb is not available,
substitute it with another of like properties,
that also shares the same planetary and elemental rulers.

—SCOTT CUNNINGHAM, *MAGICAL HERBALISM*

Sometimes you just can't get your hands on an herb that is called for in a spell, ritual, or charm. While I have focused on easy-to-find botanicals and herbs in this book, I do realize that you probably have other books on herb magic. So, I figured an herbal substitution list may come in handy. Common sense applies here. If you are working with toxic plants, please be very careful and keep them well away from children and foodstuffs. Yes, I know I've said that before, but it certainly bears repeating.

As for myself, I tend to roll my eyes at magical books that list dramatic and mysterious ingredients. While the spellwork in some tomes may be solid, the ingredients list may be incredibly challenging, expensive, unsafe, or ridiculous. In the following inventory, the spell ingredient substitutions are all natural or botanical materials. While researching this topic, I wasn't too surprised to notice that tobacco is considered an acceptable alternative to the most toxic of plants, such as belladonna and aconite. There is a certain logic to this, since tobacco products cause so many health problems.

If using tobacco makes you uncomfortable, try working with nicotiana *(Nicotiana)*. This beautiful, annual flowering tobacco is found in most garden centers and nurseries.

If you can find the pale-green variety, it is a bonus for your magical gardens, as the flowers are very fragrant at night. Also, it is worth mentioning again that yarrow *(Achillea)* is an all-purpose magical herb as well. (I have always considered the flowering yarrow to be the herbal equivalent of the multipurpose white spell candle.) Following this list of herbal substitutions, you'll also find an accompanying spell. Happy casting!

Spell Ingredient Herbal Substitution List

Aconite: Tobacco or the flowering tobacco *(Nicotiana)*

Ambergris: Vanilla beans

Angelica: Marigold or calendula

Bergamot: Bee balm flowers, or try loose-leaf Earl Grey tea

Belladonna: Tobacco or the flowering tobacco *(Nicotiana)*

Betony: Lamb's ears

Blood: Apple cider or apple juice

Camphor: Eucalyptus

Cassia: Cinnamon

Chamomile: White daisies

Cinquefoil: Clover

Citron: An equal part of lemon peel and orange peel

Citronella: Scented geraniums

Cypress: Juniper or pine needles

Deer's tongue: Sweet woodruff *(Asperula odorata)*

Drawing powder: Powdered sugar

Frankincense: Copal, pine resin

Galangal: Fresh ginger root

Graveyard dirt: Mullein

Heliotrope: Chicory

Holly foliage or berries: Snapdragons

Honey: Real maple syrup

Hyssop: Lavender

Jasmine: Rose

John the Conqueror root: St. John's wort (foliage and flowers)

Laurel: Bay leaf

Lemongrass: Lemon balm *(Melissa)* or fresh grated lemon peel

Mace: Nutmeg

Mandrake root: Peony roots

Mineral oil: Extra virgin olive oil

Mistletoe: Mint or sage, or sphagnum moss (as it's also a parasite that grows on trees)

Mullein: Lamb's ears

Neroli: Tangerine, or orange peel

Nettles: The thistle from the dried cone of a coneflower *(Echinacea)*

Orange blossoms: Fresh grated orange peel

Orris root: The petals of the iris flower

Patchouli: Oak moss

Peppermint: Spearmint

Periwinkle: Morning glory vines and flowers

Pine needles: Rosemary

Rose hips: Rose petals or leaves

Rue: Hydrangea blossoms or bark

St. John's wort: Witch hazel

Saffron: Orange peel or crocus

Sandalwood: Frankincense

Spikenard: Cedar

Sulfur: Tobacco or the flowering tobacco *(Nicotiana)*

Sunflower: Brown-eyed Susan

Sweet grass: Sage

Thyme: Rosemary

Valerian: Catnip

Vervain: Flowering verbena

Wild violet: Pansy or viola

Wine: Grape juice

Wolfsbane (Aconite): Garlic

Wormwood: Yarrow

Spell for Herbal Substitutions

Here is a spell you can try when you have to substitute one botanical for another. You will need one white (our all-purpose color) tealight candle and the herb you are using as a substitute.

Before working this spell, prepare all of the other spell supplies. Then repeat this opening charm before you begin your specific spellwork. Just think of this as your opening spell. Light the tealight and then say:

There are times in a spell when an herb or two you must switch,
So I'll use this handy charm written by the Garden Witch.
I swap one herb for another, and it will work out fine,
Now I seal the herb magic up, with the sound of this rhyme.

At this point, continue to work your original herb magic with the different botanicals you have chosen. It will work beautifully.

I could be content if the world should think
I had scarce looked upon any other book than that of nature.

—ROBERT BOYLE

BIBLIOGRAPHY

Ban Breathnach, Sarah. *Simple Abundance: A Daybook of Comfort and Joy.* New York: Warner Books, 1995.

Bartlett, John. *Bartlett's Familiar Quotations.* Justin Kaplan, general ed. Sixteenth edition. Boston, MA: Little, Brown and Co., 1992.

Beyerl, Paul. *The Master Book of Herbalism.* Custer, WA: Phoenix Publishing, 1984.

Bremness, Lesley. *The Complete Book of Herbs.* New York: Penguin Books, 1988.

Cabot, Laurie, with Tom Cowan. *Power of the Witch.* New York: Delta Books, 1989.

Culpeper, Nicholas. *Culpeper's Color Herbal.* Edited by David Potterton. New York: Sterling Publishing, 1983.

Cunningham, Scott. *Cunningham's Encyclopedia of Magical Herbs.* St. Paul, MN: Llewellyn Publications, 1985.

———. *Magical Herbalism: The Secret Craft of the Wise.* St. Paul, MN: Llewellyn Publications, 1983.

Dugan, Ellen. *7 Days of Magic: Spells Charms & Correspondences for the Bewitching Week.* St. Paul, MN: Llewellyn Publications, 2004.

———. *Elements of Witchcraft: Natural Magick for Teens.* St. Paul, MN: Llewellyn Publications, 2003.

———. *Garden Witchery: Magick from the Ground Up.* St. Paul, MN: Llewellyn Publications, 2003.

Dugan, Ellen, contributor. *Llewellyn's 2005 Herbal Almanac.* "Herbal Bouquets for Weddings and Handfastings." St. Paul, MN: Llewellyn Publications, 2004.

———. *Llewellyn's 2004 Magical Almanac.* "Money Magic." St. Paul, MN: Llewellyn Publications, 2003.

Elliott, Charles, ed. *The Quotable Gardener.* New York: Lyons Press, 1999.

Gallagher, Anne Marie. *The Spells Bible: The Definitive Guide to Enchantments.* Cincinnati, OH: Walking Stick Press, 2003.

Gilmer, Maureen. *The Gardener's Way: A Daybook of Acts and Affirmations.* Chicago, IL: Contemporary Books, 2001.

Greer, John Michael. *Natural Magic: Potions and Powers from the Magical Garden.* St. Paul, MN: Llewellyn Publications, 2000.

Hersey, Jean. *The Woman's Day Book of Annuals and Perennials.* New York: Simon and Schuster, 1977.

Houdret, Jessica. *Practical Herb Gardening.* London: Anness Publishing, 2003.

Morrison, Dorothy, contributor. *Llewellyn's 2004 Witches' Datebook.* "Swifting of Energy." St. Paul, MN: Llewellyn Publications, 2003.

Muir, Ada. *Healing Herbs & Health Foods of the Zodiac.* St. Paul, MN: Llewellyn Publications, 1993.

Nahmad, Claire. *Earth Magic: A Wisewoman's Guide to Herbal, Astrological, and Other Folk Wisdom.* Rochester, VT: Destiny Books, 1994.

———. *Garden Spells: An Enchanting Collection of Victorian Wisdom.* Philadelphia, PA: Running Press, 1994.

Norfolk, Donald. *The Soul Garden: Creating Green Spaces for Inner Growth & Spiritual Renewal.* Woodstock, NY: Overlook Press, 2002.

Paterson, Jacqueline Memory. *Tree Wisdom: The Definitive Guidebook to the Myth, Folklore and Healing Powers of Trees.* San Francisco, CA: Thorsons, 1996.

Penczak, Christopher. *The Inner Temple of Witchcraft: Magick, Meditation and Psychic Development.* St. Paul, MN: Llewellyn Publications, 2002.

Picton, Margaret. *The Book of Magical Herbs: Herbal History, Mystery & Folklore.* Hauppauge, NY: Barron's, 2000.

Raymond, Dick. *Garden Way's Joy of Gardening.* Troy, NY: Garden Way, 1982.

Roth, Sally. *Country Living Gardener: The Successful Herb Gardener.* New York: Hearst Books, 2001.

Telesco, Patricia. *A Victorian Grimoire.* St. Paul, MN: Llewellyn Publications, 1992.

Vitale, Alice Thoms. *Leaves: In Myth, Magic & Medicine.* New York: Stewart, Tabori & Chang, 1997.

Webster, Richard. *Candle Magic for Beginners.* St. Paul, MN: Llewellyn Publications, 2004.

Whiteman, Robin. *Brother Cadfael's Herb Garden.* New York: Bullfinch Press, 1997.

Websites

Culinary Cafe, "Spice & Herb Encyclopedia," http://www. culinarycafe.com.

INDEX

To Write to the Author

If you wish to contact the author or would like more information about this book, please write to the author in care of Llewellyn Worldwide and we will forward your request. Both the author and publisher appreciate hearing from you and learning of your enjoyment of this book and how it has helped you. Llewellyn Worldwide cannot guarantee that every letter written to the author can be answered, but all will be forwarded. Please write to:

Ellen Dugan
℅ Llewellyn Worldwide
2143 Wooddale Drive, Dept. 978-0-7387-0837-9
Woodbury, Minnesota 55125-2989, U.S.A.

Please enclose a self-addressed stamped envelope for reply,
or $1.00 to cover costs. If outside U.S.A., enclose
international postal reply coupon.

Many of Llewellyn's authors have websites with additional information and resources.
For more information, please visit our website at
http://www.llewellyn.com